PRAISE FOR

The Fed Unbound

"A fascinating and deep analysis of what has gone wrong
with the American financial system. Lev Menand peels back
the layers of mythology and hagiography surrounding the
Federal Reserve to reveal just another government agency
that fell in love with deregulation and now struggles with the
consequences. The rise and rise of the repo market is central
to how a stable and well-functioning financial system became
so precarious. This is a brilliant fresh perspective on the
Federal Reserve. Lev Menand is the most important new voice
on central banking and finance today."

SIMON JOHNSON,
professor at MIT Sloan and coauthor of
*13 Bankers: The Wall Street Takeover and the
Next Financial Meltdown*

"No American institution is more important, or more
opaque to the outsider, than the Fed. Now, Lev Menand
has somehow, magically, made its functioning, its history,
its limitations, and its possible futures completely lucid,
even for the nonmathematically inclined, and, along the
way, managed to sound several alarms about the risks even
the most well-meaning opaque institution presents to
democracy."

ADAM GOPNIK,
author of *A Thousand Small Sanities:
The Moral Adventure of Liberalism*

COLUMBIA GLOBAL REPORTS
NEW YORK

The Fed Unbound
Central Banking in a Time of Crisis

Lev Menand

The Fed Unbound
Central Banking in a Time of Crisis
Copyright © 2022 by Lev Menand
All rights reserved

Published by Columbia Global Reports
91 Claremont Avenue, Suite 515
New York, NY 10027
globalreports.columbia.edu
facebook.com/columbiaglobalreports
@columbiaGR

Library of Congress Cataloging-in-Publication Data

Names: Menand, Lev, author.
Title: The fed unbound : central banking in a time of crisis / by Lev Menand.
Description: New York, NY : Columbia Global Reports, [2022] | Includes
    bibliographical references.
Identifiers: LCCN 2021059231 (print) | LCCN 2021059232 (ebook) | ISBN
    9781735913704 (paperback) | ISBN 9781735913711 (ebook)
Subjects: LCSH: Board of Governors of the Federal Reserve System (U.S.) | Federal
    Reserve banks--United States. | United States--Economic policy--21st century. |
    COVID-19 Pandemic, 2020---Economic aspects--United States.
Classification: LCC HG2565 .M46 2022 (print) | LCC HG2565 (ebook) | DDC
    332.1/10973--dc23/eng/20220107
LC record available at https://lccn.loc.gov/2021059231
LC ebook record available at https://lccn.loc.gov/2021059232

Book design by Strick&Williams
Map design by Jeffrey L. Ward
Author photograph by Emily Menand

Printed in the United States of America

For Emily,
with unbounded love
and affection

CONTENTS

Preface

During the summer of 2007, the US financial system began to break down. At first, the parts that gave out were minor and unimportant. In July, two obscure hedge funds run by the Wall Street broker dealer Bear Stearns collapsed. They lost nearly all of their investors' money. In August, the French financial conglomerate BNP Paribas blocked withdrawals from three of its investment vehicles due to the "complete evaporation of liquidity" in certain segments of the US mortgage market. Policymakers on both sides of the Atlantic were stunned. Six months later, Bear Stearns itself was on the verge of collapse. Within a year, more and bigger pieces of the financial system had stopped working, a panic had broken out, and dozens of large companies were hurtling towards the abyss.

A climax arrived on September 15, 2008. Lehman Brothers, one of the most profitable firms on Wall Street, filed for bankruptcy. In its court filing, Lehman cited $613 billion of liabilities, by far the most of any bankrupt company in history. Given the role that Lehman played in the US economy—circulating

money between households and businesses like a heart pumps
blood around a body—a wave of similar failures would almost
certainly have meant widespread business closures, job losses,
and another Great Depression or worse.

That we did not experience such a collapse is due in large
part to the efforts of a single institution, the Federal Reserve.
The Fed, as it is usually known, scrambled frantically in 2008
to keep the gears turning and the blood flowing. It did its traditional work of lowering overnight interest rates, bringing them
down to near zero. It also took a series of extraordinary actions,
crossing "red lines," stretching its legal authorities, and using its
balance sheet to lend to financial enterprises of all sorts. Ultimately, with support from Congress and the Treasury Department, it staved off disaster.

And yet, today, the Fed remains stuck in emergency mode. In
March 2020, a second panic broke out, triggering an even larger
Fed response. Meanwhile, the malfunctioning that began in 2007
spawned a series of further crises—economic and political—that
are reducing economic security, widening wealth inequality,
and damaging American democracy. As these crises worsen,
the Fed continues to take on more responsibilities and further
expand its purview.

Few saw this coming. Indeed, a decade ago, following Lehman's bankruptcy, many suspected that we had reached the
end of a "Second Gilded Age," a multi-decade period char-
acterized by a large and expanding financial sector and rising
inequality. They predicted that the financial sector would contract and inequality would subside. The Fed, too, they assumed,
would go back to normal. Now, however, it seems clear that the
acute panic in 2008 was just the beginning of a new phase, one

14   in which the government's part in facilitating sprawling financial markets became explicit, and the Fed, an organization built for limited regulatory purposes, emerged as a site of enormous economic and political power.

Importantly, this shift is not unique to the United States. Japan experienced its own 2008-style breakdown in the 1990s, which was followed by an extended period of economic stagnation. In response, the Bank of Japan pioneered many of the unorthodox methods that the Fed has since tried here, including massive balance sheet expansion. Today, the Bank of Japan holds assets worth over 700 trillion yen (approximately $6.5 trillion), more than ten times the amount it held before the 1990s measured as a percentage of Japan's annual economic output.

In Europe, the transformation has been even starker. The 2010s were a decade of extreme monetary dysfunction and rolling depressions in multiple countries. The European Central Bank, known as the ECB, spearheaded a host of unprecedented measures to prevent the "eurozone" (the collection of European states that use the euro as their currency) from disintegrating. Many of the ECB's efforts continue still, including its monthly purchases of tens of billions of euros' worth of public and private sector securities.

But if this is a revolution, it's of a very odd sort. As we will see, the rise of Atlas-like central banks engaged in perpetual crisis management is the product of a conservative impulse. Today's Fed officials are not aiming for radical change. They are trying to return things as much as possible to the status quo ante, to the way things were before the summer of 2007. They are trying to preserve a system of globalized finance that their

predecessors played a leading role in constructing and that
imploded spectacularly fourteen years ago.

Unfortunately, despite their herculean efforts, this system
remains economically and politically unstable. It undermines
the legal framework governing money and finance and threatens
our democracy. Among its shortcomings, it depends on central
bank actions that, though designed to avoid worse outcomes,
transfer wealth to the financial sector and increase inequality.

This book makes a case for fundamental reform. It offers
a comprehensive look at the Fed and its growing role in our
society and argues that legislative gridlock and the erosion of
our banking laws has led the Fed to take on responsibilities for
which it was not designed. It then explores some of the consequences of this dynamic and suggests better approaches to
managing the economy. Rather than continue on our current
trajectory, treating the symptoms of an inadequate macroeconomic and financial architecture with a continuous dose of central bank medicine, I argue that it is time to cure the disease by
rebuilding our fiscal and monetary infrastructure and placing
our economy on more solid ground.

Introduction

It is a basic principle of American law that Congress has the power of the purse. "No money shall be drawn from the United States Treasury," the Constitution tells us, "but in consequence of appropriations made by law." This restriction is the reason why federal agencies shut down when legislators are unable to pass annual appropriation bills. It is also why people sometimes worry that the US will default on its debts: the Treasury Department can only pay the country's creditors when Congress authorizes it to do so.

But Congress is not the only part of the federal government that can put money to work. There is another government organization that also has the ability to disburse funds: the Federal Reserve. The Fed is run by a seven-member Board of Governors headquartered in Washington, DC, with twelve federally chartered banks, known as Federal Reserve Banks, located around the country. Established by Congress in 1913, the Fed possesses what we might call the "power of the printing press." It can create money out of thin air. And the Fed operates independently from

The Marriner S. Eccles Federal Reserve Board Building,
Washington, DC

the rest of the government, meaning that it can create as much money as it sees fit and use this money without prior approval from Congress or the president.

Most people do not think about the Fed or its power to create money. One reason for this is that when Congress created the Fed, it wrote laws carefully restricting how the Fed uses its printing press. The Fed is not permitted to raise an army or fund a space program. Its job is to regulate the money supply—to make sure there is enough money in the economy for everyone else to use—not to use money itself. The Fed is authorized to put new money into circulation in only two ways: by buying financial assets and by lending. And Congress limited the sorts of financial assets the Fed can buy and the kinds of entities the Fed can lend to. As a result, Congress has long directed government resources, with the Fed's balance sheet in the background.

18   This all started to change about fourteen years ago. Facing a severe financial crisis, the Fed used its power to create money to avert an economic meltdown. In March of 2008, it lent $29 billion to prevent the bankruptcy of Bear Stearns, the troubled Wall Street securities dealer. Neither Congress nor the White House was involved in making the loan. One prominent legislator later admitted that he had no idea the Fed even had the authority. (Neither, he said, did most of his colleagues.) The Fed had not invoked the relevant provision in over seventy years.*

Six months later, in September of 2008, a group of Fed officials went to Capitol Hill to brief legislators on a plan to lend $80 billion to rescue a failing insurance conglomerate, AIG. They got a frosty reception. AIG was not a government-chartered bank, the type of business the Fed was designed to support during economic contractions. Besides, the chairman of the House Finance Committee wanted to know, where was the Fed planning to get $80 billion? Steeped in the traditional division of labor between Congress and the Fed, the chairman failed to realize that the Fed could lend without drawing on the Treasury at all. The Fed could simply create new money at a keystroke.

By year-end, the Fed had committed $123 billion to save AIG. It had also established several ad hoc lending programs designed to stabilize other financial companies whose distress threatened to bring down government-chartered banks and

---

* The largest loan the Fed had previously made using this authority was $300,000, which it lent to Smith & Corona, the typewriter company, in 1933. Prior to 2008, the total of the Fed's emergency lending to firms without bank charters *in its history* was just $1.5 million, all of which it lent during a period, the Great Depression, when nearly a third of the country's banks closed their doors.

other businesses. The Fed even lent half a trillion dollars to foreign central banks like the Bank of England, the Bank of Japan, and the European Central Bank so that these institutions could backstop financial businesses in Europe and Asia.

Although the Fed's extraordinary actions saved us from a second Great Depression, they were not enough to prevent millions of Americans from losing their homes, jobs, and sense of economic security. Faced with the prospect of a slow and painful recovery, Fed officials continued to improvise. In January of 2009, the Fed began to purchase bundles of home loans known as mortgage-backed securities (MBS) through a program the press took to calling "quantitative easing," or QE. In 2010 and 2012, with overnight interest rates near zero, and the financial system still unable to jump-start economic growth, the Fed launched two further rounds of QE—QE2 and QE3— expanding its purchases to include government-issued Treasury bonds. Fed officials hoped that by buying these securities they would stimulate borrowing and lending and, consequently, spending.* It wasn't an ideal response to economic stagnation; a by-product of buying these securities was higher asset prices, which disproportionately benefited people who owned assets. But in the face of anemic credit creation by banks and inadequate fiscal spending by Congress, it was the best Fed officials could do with the tools they had.

By 2014, the Fed had amassed a portfolio worth over $2 trillion. At this point, Fed policy was supposed to return to

---

* For example, they expected buying mortgage-backed securities to lower the servicing costs for people with mortgages, pushing down their monthly interest payments. Lower payments, in turn, would mean more money that homeowners could use to buy goods and services.

20   normal. Having put out the fires, and turned the economy back
     toward growth, the Fed would wind down its balance sheet and
     resume its traditional work of supervising banks and adjusting
     short-term interest rates. But the crisis that had begun six years
     earlier wasn't really over. The private financial sector, it turned
     out, could still not stand on its own two feet. In September of
     2019, as the Fed continued to sell off the assets it had accumu-
     lated, financial markets cracked up, prompting another major
     lending program for Wall Street broker dealers. Although little
     noticed outside of the financial press, by year end, the Fed's out-
     standing loans to these firms exceeded $250 billion.

     Six months later, the Fed was still trying to close out this
     program when the COVID-19 pandemic triggered a fresh eco-
     nomic downturn. Stock indices fell 20 percent in two weeks. In
     a desperate rush to survive, highly leveraged securities dealers
     and hedge funds began dumping assets on the market for what-
     ever price buyers were willing to pay. On top of a global pan-
     demic and economywide shutdown, the US was suddenly facing
     another financial panic.

     Having learned in 2008 just how wrong a panic can go, in
     2020 the Fed acted with lightning speed and at even greater
     scale. It added $3 trillion to its balance sheet, one-third of which
     it loaned to financial firms that were not government-chartered
     banks. It used the remaining two-thirds to buy government
     bonds and mortgage-backed securities, the sorts of securi-
     ties financial firms were selling. In just one month, Fed officials
     deployed almost as much money as Congress allocates in a year.

     The Fed also expanded the variety of borrowers who
     could access its emergency programs. In this decision, legis-
     lators played an important role. On March 27, 2020, Congress

passed the Coronavirus Aid, Relief, and Economic Security (CARES) Act, authorizing the Fed to set up facilities to lend to medium-sized enterprises, state and local governments, and large corporations—the sorts of entities that usually receive government loans from agencies like the Small Business Administration and Treasury Department using money appropriated by Congress. Between April and December, the Fed lent $40 billion to a range of non-financial borrowers, including Apple, AT&T, a gym operator based in California, a nationwide energy conglomerate with thousands of oil and gas properties, New York's Metropolitan Transit Authority, and the State of Illinois.

Fearing that these initiatives would not be enough to keep the financial system operating smoothly and the economy growing, the Fed also restarted QE. Its latest iteration—QE Infinity—rapidly surpassed previous rounds and, as of October 2021, was still pumping $120 billion per month into financial markets.* As a result, although the US economy is still smaller than it was projected to be before the pandemic, stocks, bonds, and real estate have all reached record high valuations, with the S&P 500 index a full 40 percent above its pre-pandemic peak.

The result has been nothing short of a transformation in the Fed's role in our society. Not only have its unprecedented actions helped once again to avert economic collapse, but they have also changed what members of Congress and members of the public expect of the country's central bankers. Today, the

---

* On November 3, 2021, the Fed announced that it would "taper" the pace of its purchases by $15 billion per month, meaning that QE Infinity would stop expanding in July 2022. On December 15, the Fed accelerated this taper, doubling its pace and bringing forward the date of final purchases to March.

22   Fed is no longer just managing the money supply by administering the banking system. It is fighting persistent economic and financial crises by using its balance sheet like an emergency government credit bureau or national investment authority—creating new money to backstop financial firms, expand financial markets, and invest in businesses and municipalities. To provide a sense of just how stark this transformation has been, chart 1.1 shows the Fed's balance sheet both before and after September 2008. While Fed officials still lack the power to fund government programs as legislators do, they can nevertheless direct loans and design asset purchase plans in ways that greatly influence the course of economic activity.

Awed by the strength of today's Fed, a range of interest groups, public intellectuals, and policy think tanks are now calling for it to use its printing press to address other crises facing the country. They propose Fed programs to support state and local governments, make transfer payments to individuals, finance green energy projects, and restrict credit to polluting industries. If the Fed can create money to save financial firms and boost asset prices, surely, these advocates argue, the Fed can use its powers to directly tackle problems hurting ordinary people.

Are they right? Should the Fed take on these tasks? And why has the Fed started using its printing press to rescue financial firms and buy financial assets?

Any attempt to answer these questions immediately raises more basic questions, like: What *is* the Fed's job? And why does the Fed have the power to create money? These questions are not simply for economists, bankers, and policy experts. The Fed is a public institution. And its power to create money affects our democracy and the distribution of wealth and power in our

CHART 1.1
The Fed's Balance Sheet (in trillions of US$)

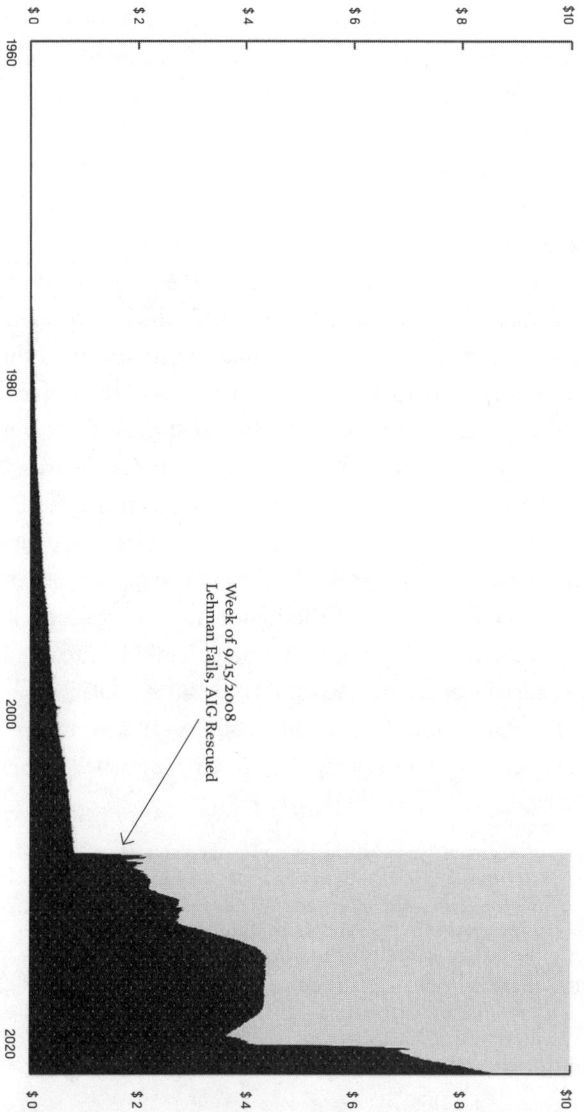

Week of 9/15/2008
Lehman Fails, AIG Rescued

$10 $8 $6 $4 $2 $0

1960   1980   2000   2020

$0 $2 $4 $6 $8 $10

Source: Federal Reserve Board; Federal Reserve Bank of St. Louis

24   society. Current debates about the Fed tend to focus on technical issues, overlooking the larger stakes for American politics. And even many Fed officials are confused about the Fed's statutory mission and legal architecture. They misunderstand its mandate and fail to appreciate how its expanding scope over the past fourteen years is a product of profound and continuing deficiencies in our economic and financial system.

This book aims to open up and deepen the public conversation about the Fed. It attempts to demystify the organization's recent activities and illuminate the stakes of its recent actions for our society. It also explains why Congress built the Fed in the first place. The Fed, I argue, was not designed to do whatever it takes to keep the economy out of recession, or to tackle pressing social problems using its printing press. It was designed for a limited purpose—to administer the banking system. Congress set up a decentralized network of publicly chartered, privately owned banks to issue most of the money in the economy. The Fed's designated role is to ensure that these banks create enough money to keep the economy growing at its full potential.

The Fed has come "unbound," that is, it has taken on tasks for which it was not designed,* in large part because of a

---

* It is common in central banking circles to invoke the story of Odysseus, the Greek hero who tied himself to the mast of his ship to avoid the temptation to alter his course. In the analogy, legislatures construct independent central banks like the Fed to limit their ability to overissue money to pay their bills—they bind themselves to the mast. But this is not the analogy I am drawing here. This book's title invokes the idea of binding in a different sense: Congress bound the Fed to perform a limited role so that it could do its job effectively (and so other parts of the government could do theirs as well).

structural problem that emerged many years before 2007: the rise of firms that create money like banks but that do not have government charters to do so. The Fed was not built to manage a monetary system that relies on these financial enterprises, but unless it is willing to risk a Second Great Depression, it is often pressed to rescue them when they get into trouble.

What should we do about this? Faced with widespread dysfunction across the federal government, many commentators, including many members of Congress, embrace the new Fed and argue for expanding its role even further. The appeal is easy to see. The Fed is well staffed and well funded. It can act quickly, with few procedural constraints and little chance of searching judicial review. It is not subject to the debt ceiling or other government budget rules. And it does not need to tax or borrow before making loans or buying financial assets.

But relying on the Fed to handle tasks traditionally performed by legislators and other administrators is shortsighted. The Fed, because of the way it is organized, is not well suited to handle these responsibilities. It is insulated from public participation, closely interconnected with banks and other financial institutions, and independent from many forms of political oversight. Given its tools and procedures, it is unlikely to ever be a progressive *deus ex machina*, fixing problems like climate change that other parts of the government fail to address. To the contrary, centralizing power into one big bank runs the risk of creating a Supreme Court—like body, shielded from popular accountability, that governs the economy in ways that, because of the tasks it is called upon to perform, disproportionately benefit certain groups. If our goal is to create a more

26   equitable and inclusive society, we need Congress to fundamen-
tally reform our financial system and take the lead on crafting
macroeconomic policy.

Plan of the Book

The rest of this book develops and defends this argument.
Chapter 1 returns to the start of the pandemic and examines
the Fed in action. Chapters 2 and 3 turn to the Fed's history
and legal architecture to better understand how the Fed came
to play such a big role in our economy. Chapter 2 starts with
the basics. It explains how money works in the United States.
The Fed plays an important role, but not nearly as important
as you might think. That is because, although the Fed issues
our paper money, it does not issue our "deposit money." The US
government outsources that power to publicly chartered, privately owned banks—banks like Wells Fargo, JPMorgan Chase,
and Bank of America. Deposit money is what employers use to
pay salaries (e.g., "direct deposits") and what households use to
pay credit card bills. Cash—the paper notes the Fed issues along
with the metal coins issued by the US Mint—plays a compara-
tively minor role in our economy. Cash is something that banks
promise to give their customers when they ask for it, but that
their customers rarely ask for and seldom use.

Chapter 3 shows how Congress designed the Fed to make
the banking system work better for ordinary households and
businesses. The Fed's primary job is to oversee banks and provide them with access to cash when people want it or need it,
to ensure that there is enough money—cash and deposits—to
keep the nation's resources productively employed. Legislators were especially concerned with fluctuations in economic

activity. When the economy shrinks, either due to seasonal factors or one-off events, banks reduce their deposits by cutting back their lending. Sometimes these slowdowns prompt bank runs and failures, causing deep and lasting recessions. The Fed is built to counteract these tendencies by regulating banks, lending to them, and helping them lend to everyone else.

Chapter 4 examines the forces that have caused the Fed increasingly to act outside the banking system. It argues that the primary cause of the Fed's transformation since 2008 is something that began many decades earlier: the rise of "shadow banks," firms that, like banks, create alternative forms of money, but, unlike banks, lack a charter to do so. Bear Stearns and Lehman Brothers are two famous examples. The Fed does not have the power to regulate these firms and their alternative forms of money in the way that it regulates banks and bank deposits. Nonetheless, the Fed has repeatedly lent to shadow banks in order to stop runs on their deposit substitutes, as these instruments are a critical part of today's money supply. One of the side effects of the Fed's efforts has been to facilitate more shadow banking by creating the expectation that the government stands behind shadow banks just as it stands behind banks. The Fed's efforts, and the damage inflicted by shadow banks in 2008, have also created the conditions (and the political imperatives) for the Fed to turn its balance sheet to new ends, spurring calls for it to take on issues that normally legislators or other agencies would tackle.

Chapter 5 examines the dangers of relying on the Fed to hold our economic and financial system together. It argues that today's expanded Fed is not only out of step with the Federal Reserve Act, the law from which its power derives, but also that

28   it leads to suboptimal policy outcomes. Worse, expanding the Fed's role risks short-circuiting the proper functioning of democratic politics. When the Fed uses its balance sheet to address economic problems, it unavoidably helps certain groups, such as homeowners and the financial sector, alleviating political pressures (from these groups) that might otherwise lead Congress to enact new legislation to stimulate economic growth.

Chapter 6 suggests a way forward. While bankers and central bankers must certainly do their part to tackle economic challenges, including climate change, it would be a mistake to rely on them to carry out functions better suited to Congress or other administrative agencies. Durable policy progress requires political action: a more democratic legislative process and a more accountable executive branch. It also requires new laws and institutions. Two areas need attention. First, we need a better approach to managing the business cycle. Congress should play a bigger role in responding to macroeconomic shocks and create more fiscal tools, such as automatic transfer payments, to reduce the country's reliance on monetary adjustments that, as we will see, disproportionately benefit the financial sector. Checks from the Treasury Department, for example, such as those authorized by Congress three times since 2020, can more quickly, equitably, and effectively stimulate the economy to operate at full capacity. Second, we need a better monetary infrastructure. Congress and agency administrators should end unauthorized money creation. If we want to stabilize the economy, we need fewer shadow banks and more nonprofit banks, not a bigger central bank that sits on top of an ever-expanding private financial sector. Efforts to reform our

banking laws in the wake of the 2008 financial crisis focused on
reducing leverage, enhancing transparency, and protecting consumers and investors from abusive and fraudulent practices. It is
time to take these efforts a step further. Congress should pursue
structural reform, reworking the balance of power between the
financial sector and the government so that our system is efficient, equitable, and inclusive.

The Fed and the Pandemic

In March of 2020, as schools and businesses around the country shut down, the Fed went into overdrive. Alongside COVID-19, another disease was spreading, and its progress could not be halted using N-95s or social distancing. This disease moved faster than any virus, and, if history was any guide, threatened harms as profound as the pandemic itself: a rapid contraction in the money supply and breakdown of our basic economic machinery, the infrastructure that allows us to produce trillions of dollars of goods and services each year. We were facing a financial panic.

The Pandemic Panic

The trouble began on Monday, March 9. Following a weekend of growing fears about whether the spread of COVID-19 would lead businesses to miss interest payments and default on their debts, stock markets dropped nearly 10 percent in one day. Bond prices also crashed. Between March 3 and March 23, the "spreads" on high quality debt issued by large corporations

rose from 1 percent to 4 percent, meaning that investors were
demanding four times as much interest from companies to
cover the risk of default. Firms already carrying high debt loads
fared even worse: spreads on their bonds spiked to 10 percent.*

But not all shocks of this sort lead to *panics*. Drops in asset
prices, even rapid drops, are an unavoidable feature of a capi-
talist economy in which things are easily bought and sold by
a wide range of actors. Pandemics, wars, natural disasters, and
coups occur from time to time, changing the value of businesses
and other investments. Asset prices can also shift rapidly when
people get carried away with irrational exuberance, bidding up
real estate or stocks, since the resulting bubbles sometimes
burst suddenly.

Often the consequences of a fall in asset prices following
a shock are fairly limited. The people who own the deflated
assets lose some of their wealth. As a result, they pare back their
spending, putting a mild drag on economic activity. Everyone
else moves on. This is what happened, for example, in Canada
during the 2008 financial crisis—prices for homes dropped
modestly, but no Canadian financial institutions failed, and
there was no major damage to the wider economy.** This is also
what happened in the United States in 2000, following the collapse of the "tech bubble," during which the stock prices for
internet companies reached record highs.

* At this rate, a business borrowing $100 for ten years would owe $100 in
interest just to cover the risk of default, a cost that on its own could spell the
end of the road.

** Indeed, despite being subject to many economic shocks, Canadians have
never experienced a full-blown financial panic at any point in their history.
The United States, meanwhile, has had over a dozen.

32   Panics go beyond a mere repricing of assets. In a panic, a shock causes an initial round of selling, which itself gives rise to further rounds of selling—a downward spiral that can lead the entire economy to collapse. Panics are usually the product of structural vulnerabilities in the financial system. Indeed, nearly every panic in American history, including 2020's pandemic panic, has been caused by a particular type of structural vulnerability, one involving companies that issue liabilities that function as money. These companies take government-issued cash and promise to pay it back on demand, or within a very short period of time. People treat these promises as indistinguishable from cash. We sometimes call them "money claims," and our economy relies on them to function.

The most common money claim, issued by banks, is known as a deposit. Think of an account at Chase or Bank of America. If you open an app, go to an ATM, or log in online, you can check your account balance. To you, the account holder, this balance is the same as cash. To you, it's actually better than cash: most people would rather store value and transact using these balances. But cash and deposits are two separate *kinds* of money. The bank does not hold cash on your behalf, like a restaurant stores your coat while you are eating dinner. Nor does the bank hold much cash at all. Instead, the bank invests in all sorts of long-term, hard-to-sell financial assets like bonds, mortgage loans, and credit card receivables.

As we will see in the following chapters, the people who designed the American banking system assumed that only chartered banks would issue money claims; indeed, they wrote laws to try to make certain this would be the case. But these laws were poorly designed and poorly enforced. Although they are

intended to prohibit financial institutions that are not regulated
as banks from issuing deposits, over the past several decades
an increasing number of such institutions—so-called "shadow
banks"—have skirted the restrictions by creating a variety of
alternative forms of money.

Shadow banks come in all shapes and sizes: some are structured as mutual funds for retail investors, others deal in financial
instruments on Wall Street, still others are banks based overseas, beyond the jurisdiction of US regulators. The alternative
forms of money that shadow banks issue are similarly diverse—
we will examine them more closely in chapter 4. What they all
have in common is that they are products that, while legally dis-
tinguishable from deposits, share many of the same economic
characteristics and also function as a substitute for cash.

One of the critical features that deposits and deposit alternatives share is that the people who hold them do not think of
themselves as "investors" in the companies that issued them.
They do not think, for example, that they have loaned money
to the institution and that the loan comes due the next day.
(Do you consider yourself an investor in your bank?) Nor do
the companies treat these balances as ordinary borrowings, in
which repayment is expected at the conclusion of the loan's
term. They count on most people to roll them over—to keep
the arrangement in place. Banks and shadow banks know that,
on any given day, some people may ask for cash, but banks and
shadow banks expect that the number of people who ask for
cash will, over time, equal the number of people who bring cash
back again.

In a panic, the music stops. Suddenly, the people with deposits (or other money claims) change their minds. They worry

34   that the bank or shadow bank that issued the claim might find itself in financial trouble, unable to fulfill its promise to pay cash (or some other form of money) on demand. And rather than wait to find out, they stop rolling over. When everyone does this at once, the issuers are in a bind: they have to start selling their assets to raise cash to make good on their money claims. This is called a fire sale. When everyone starts selling assets without regard to the price, and there are no new buyers eager to step in, prices plummet. As this happens, and as more people become aware that it is happening, more people worry that money claim issuers will be unable to make good on their claims and so they, too, ask for a safer form of money. The result is that the system in which private firms supply most of the money in the economy starts to fall apart.

That is what happened the week of March 9, 2020. The drop in the value of assets caused by COVID-19 led businesses and other large investors to lose confidence in the money claims issued by shadow banks. As shadow banks started selling assets to satisfy withdrawals, prices continued to plummet. As falling prices forced levered speculators to unwind their positions,* more firms were drawn into the spiral, adding further pressure to sell. It was another monetary conflagration—one that burned faster and brighter than the one in 2008.

The intensity of the flames caught the government off guard. Top officials, such as Jay Powell, the Fed's Chair, and

---

* A levered speculator is a person who has borrowed money to invest in financial assets. When those assets lose value, levered speculators are often forced to sell them to repay the money they have borrowed, "unwinding" their position.

Randy Quarles, its Vice Chair for Bank Supervision, had recently
argued that the government had more or less solved the problems that had triggered the global financial crisis. Quarles,
a former bank lawyer and undersecretary in the Treasury
Department, thought that the government had actually overcorrected: not only had it adequately addressed the risk of
another financial crisis, but it had put so many safeguards in
place that bank shareholders were being unfairly penalized.
Many policymakers did not imagine that another panic could
come so soon, let alone a panic that stuck so quickly and with
such little advance notice.

But despite being taken by surprise, the leading civil servants at the Fed and the Treasury Department knew what a panic
looked like. Whereas in 2008, American officials had not faced a
full-fledged domestic financial crisis in nearly eighty-five years,
many of the officials in the government in 2020 had seen one
up close. Lorie Logan, who was responsible for the day-to-day
operation of the Fed's asset purchases in 2020, started working
at the Fed's bank in New York in 1999. Nellie Liang, the Director
of the Fed's Division of Financial Stability, was a senior economist at the Fed during the run on Lehman Brothers. These officials had learned hard lessons in 2008, one of which was that
panics can cause extensive collateral damage. Another was not
to be indecisive.

On Thursday, March 12, with the panic intensifying, the
Fed acted decisively. It announced that its New York bank
would offer up to $1.5 trillion in short-term loans to a group of
twenty-four Wall Street firms known as "the primary dealers."
The primary dealers trade stocks, bonds, and derivatives. Some of

36   them are owned by large financial conglomerates like JPMorgan Chase and Goldman Sachs, which also own chartered banks. Others, including Cantor Fitzgerald, Amherst Pierpont, and Jefferies, are stand-alone operations. Still others, like Mizuho Securities, Deutsche Bank Securities, Nomura Securities, and UBS, are owned by foreign banking conglomerates.

The primary dealers trade financial instruments with other financial institutions, as well as with large investors. They have a close relationship with the Fed because they serve as its counterparties when it needs to buy or sell securities as part of its day-to-day monetary policy. But selling securities to the Fed (and others) is not the only way that the primary dealers make money. The dealers also compete with banks on the liability side of their balance sheets. In addition to borrowing from traditional investors, which is how ordinary businesses like AT&T and Walmart finance their activities, the primary dealers issue money claims that function like bank deposits. The primary dealers are a type of shadow bank.

The money claims that dealers issue are called repurchase agreements, or "repos." Although repos and bank deposits are substitutes—the firms that give dealers cash in a repo do so in lieu of depositing that cash in a bank or holding another alternative form of money—the primary dealers do not have access to the Fed programs that Congress designed to maintain public confidence in deposits. Those programs are limited by law to chartered banks subject to government banking regulation—well-known companies like the depository arms of Bank of America, Citibank, and Wells Fargo. Unable to participate alongside these banks, the primary dealers are particularly vulnerable to runs.

In March, the people doing repos with the primary dealers—pension funds, hedge funds, big industrial and technology firms, and other financial institutions—wanted out. This was extremely destabilizing. As the demand for repos suddenly plummeted, the primary dealers were forced to start selling their investment portfolios.

The Fed, by announcing its intention to provide the primary dealers with the sort of government backing that keeps banks stable, hoped to reverse this dynamic. And it worked. While total borrowing from the Fed peaked at $450 billion, the Fed's announcement itself had a calming effect: people who held alternative forms of money issued by the primary dealers (and by other dealers that looked to the primary dealers for support) interpreted the announcement as a signal that the Fed was standing behind their money claims, that the US government would not let repo-financed institutions fail.

Still, the Fed's $1.5 trillion repo backstop was not enough to halt the broader panic. There were too many other shadow banks in trouble, too many other market participants selling off their portfolios under duress.

One area of concern was overseas. Foreign companies, especially in Europe and Asia, were also in the business of issuing alternative forms of money denominated in dollars. Some even offered traditional dollar deposit accounts despite the fact that they lacked US bank charters. With asset prices falling, and the future of these firms in doubt, people holding these claims had second thoughts. They asked for a safer form of money, like a bank deposit at a US bank. To meet these obligations, foreign firms dumped billions of dollars of American stocks and bonds. The fire was getting worse.

38   On Sunday, March 15, the Fed took a page from its response to the global financial crisis.* The Fed announced that it would lend an unlimited amount of dollars to central banks in Canada, the UK, Japan, Europe, and Switzerland at bargain-basement interest rates, less than 50 basis points (half of 1 percent). The Fed would structure these loans as "swaps": the foreign central banks would buy dollars using their own currencies (such as pounds, euros, and yen), and at a future date the Fed would sell back these foreign currencies for the dollars it initially sold.

By the end of May, total uptake on the Fed's "swap lines" reached 2008 levels: nearly half a trillion dollars. To appreciate the magnitude of this program, consider some transaction-level data. The Bank of Japan, the biggest participant, borrowed $30 billion on March 17 (for eighty-four days at a rate of 0.37 percent). On Monday March 23, Japan drew another $35 billion (for seven days at a rate of 0.38 percent). The next day, it took down a massive $74 billion (for eighty-four days at a rate of 0.35 percent) and $15 billion (for seven days at a rate of 0.36 percent). On Wednesday, Thursday, and Friday of that same week, it borrowed a combined $20 billion more. Over the following three weeks it took another $100 billion, all at rates of 0.33 percent or less. Although the Fed does not report what the Bank of Japan or the other big foreign central banks did with the money they borrowed, we can be fairly confident that they lent it to various financial firms operating within their jurisdictions, firms that were experiencing runs on their dollar-denominated money claims just like those located in the United States.

* A crisis that was *global* for precisely this reason: runs on foreign financial institutions that issue dollar denominated money claims.

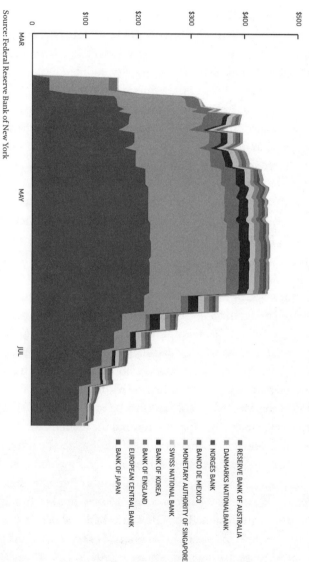

CHART 1.2
The Fed's Swap Lines (in billions of US$)

Source: Federal Reserve Bank of New York

RESERVE BANK OF AUSTRALIA
DANMARKS NATIONALBANK
NORGES BANK
BANCO DE MEXICO
MONETARY AUTHORITY OF SINGAPORE
SWISS NATIONAL BANK
BANK OF KOREA
BANK OF ENGLAND
EUROPEAN CENTRAL BANK
BANK OF JAPAN

40   Yet the panic selling continued—in part because the problems at home were not yet contained. On March 17, the Fed
finally invoked its emergency authority to lend to companies
without bank charters. Using this authority, codified in Section
13(3) of the Federal Reserve Act, requires a supermajority vote
of the Fed's board, as well as the approval of the Treasury Secretary. It also requires that the Fed report its lending to Congress
and ensure collateral sufficient to protect itself against losses.
(When the Fed uses 13(3), it is not legally allowed to lend unless
it expects it will be paid back in full.)

The Fed's first move with this emergency power was to
further support the primary dealers. It established a Primary
Dealer Credit Facility similar to one it had invented in 2008. The
facility accepted a wider range of collateral than the $1.5 trillion
repo program announced five days earlier. It offered the same
rock bottom interest rate that the Fed was already offering to
government-chartered banks. And it had no limit on the amount
of lending; the Fed would create and lend as much money as the
dealers wanted to borrow, provided they could post the appropriate collateral. Indeed, policymakers hoped that the primary
dealers would borrow not just for themselves but also on behalf of
other dealers that the Fed had not authorized to borrow directly.

The Fed also used 13(3) to move beyond the primary dealers
and their network. Two other groups of US financial companies were teetering: money market mutual funds and commercial paper issuers. Money market mutual funds offer a product
that operates a lot like a bank account. Money market funds
offer shares that are designed to maintain a stable value in nom-
inal terms over time and earn a bit of interest every month. Like
banks, money market funds do not actually hold cash to back

their account balances. Money funds are invested in a range of 41 financial assets. And when those assets lose value, people sometimes decide they would like to go back to banks. In September of 2008, one of the biggest money market funds, the Reserve Primary Fund, collapsed after Lehman Brothers filed for bankruptcy.* The problem was that the Fund owned debt issued by Lehman Brothers and if that debt turned out to be worthless, the Fund would not be able to pay back all its account holders in full. The Fund, in other words, "broke the buck": its assets stopped being worth $1 per share.

As the week of March 9 wore on, fears that falling asset prices might cause money funds to break the buck again led to a surge in net redemptions: $10 billion on Tuesday; $15 billion on Wednesday; $25 billion on Friday. The companies that managed these funds, like Goldman Sachs and the Bank of New York Mellon, quickly stepped in to help them out: Goldman bought $1 billion of assets from its Financial Square Money Market Fund and Square Prime Obligations Fund, and the Bank of New York Mellon deployed $2.1 billion to support Dreyfus Cash Management.

The other group of financial companies under pressure were firms that extend credit to consumers, often to buy cars. There is nothing inherently unstable about the consumer lending business, but some of these firms try to maximize profits by financing their activities using commercial paper (or CP, as it is commonly known) instead of raising money from long-term

---

* The Reserve Primary Fund held assets of $62.4 billion when it collapsed on September 16—making it larger than the vast majority of chartered banks in the United States at the time.

42   investors. Commercial paper is another alternative form of money, the bulk of which is issued by nonbank financial institutions. The biggest issuers as of 2018 were TD, a Canadian bank; the consumer lending division of Toyota, the car company; and ING, a Dutch financial conglomerate.

Commercial paper is a short-term debt obligation, often with a maturity less than four days. The people who buy this sort of debt—primarily money market funds, large companies, and institutional investors—are similar to the people who maintain deposit accounts: they aren't interested in bearing any credit risk. They often rely on the money to make payroll or settle other obligations. Accordingly, they will walk away at the first sign of trouble. Since money funds held a significant share of commercial paper, as the run on money funds continued during the week of March 9, the $1 trillion commercial paper market started to show strains. The fire was getting worse.

Accordingly, on March 17 and 18, the Fed opened two more facilities: the Commercial Paper Funding Facility to backstop commercial paper issuers and the Money Market Mutual Fund Liquidity Facility to backstop money funds. The Fed limited the former to $100 billion but put no limit on the latter: by April 9, total borrowing in this latter facility topped $50 billion.

These facilities were a bit different from the Primary Dealer Credit Facility. There was a risk that, by lending to some of these firms, the Fed might lose money. Accordingly, the Fed called on the Treasury Department to cover potential losses.* And the

---

* While Treasury money is federal government money just like Fed money, legally there is a difference. As noted above, when the Fed lends through its emergency authority, it cannot expect to lose money. The Treasury has access to funds that Congress has not restricted in this way.

TABLE 1.1

The Fed's Panic Prevention Facilities During the Pandemic

DATE	FACILITY	LIMIT	MAX USAGE	CREDIT RISK	TREASURY APPROVAL + REPORTING
3/12	Repurchase Operations	Up to $1.5 trillion	$441B (March 18)	Fed	No
3/15	Swap Lines	Unlimited*	$448B (May 28)	Fed	No
3/17	Commercial Paper Funding Facility (CPFF)	Unlimited	$13B (July 9)	Treasury (first $10 billion) then Fed	Yes
3/17	Primary Dealer Credit Facility (PDCF)	Unlimited	$35B (April 16)	Fed	Yes
3/18	MMF Liquidity Facility (MMLF)	Unlimited	$53B (April 9)	Treasury (first $10 billion) then Fed	Yes
3/31	Foreign and International Monetary Authorities (FIMA) Repo Facility	Unlimited	$1B (May 14)	Fed	No

* The 3/15 swap lines for the Eurozone, UK, Canada, Japan, and Switzerland were unlimited. The lines added on March 19 for Australia, Brazil, South Korea, Mexico, Singapore, and Sweden were limited to $60 billion per country and the lines added for Denmark, Norway, and New Zealand were limited to $30 billion per country. The usage figure reflects all these lines combined.

Source: Federal Reserve Board

Treasury Department heeded the call. But it wasn't simple. The Treasury does not have a printing press, nor does it have the power of the purse. It can make investments only when Congress authorizes it to do so. What to do? In recent decades, Treasury officials have figured out a way to bypass this restriction using an investment account called the Exchange Stabilization Fund. Congress created the Exchange Stabilization Fund in 1934 so that the Treasury Secretary can manage the exchange rate between dollars and foreign currencies. The Fund has a balance of many tens of billions of dollars. Amid the turmoil, Secretary Steven Mnuchin drew on the account to backstop these Fed facilities. It was not clear that he had the legal authority

44   to use the Fund in this way, but past Treasury Secretaries had already made a habit of drawing on it in emergencies, and it was not clear who was in a position to challenge his decision.

On March 19, the Fed expanded its response even further. It added swap lines with nine new counterparties: central banks in Australia, Sweden, Norway, Denmark, New Zealand, Brazil, Mexico, South Korea, and Singapore. Later, to limit any further pressure from foreign sources, the Fed expanded this global safety net by announcing a new Foreign and International Monetary Authorities Repo Facility. This program included over a hundred additional foreign central banks and accepted collateral in the form of US treasuries.[*]

The animating idea behind each of these facilities was to backstop financial firms in the money claim business—to make sure that the money they issued was (and would be viewed as) interchangeable with the money the government issued. Policymakers followed the advice of nineteenth-century financial

---

[*] The Foreign and International Monetary Authorities Repo Facility is an alternative to the swap lines that exposes the Fed to less risk of loss. In a swap, after the Fed increases the account balance of the foreign central bank, the foreign central bank lends that money to its own financial system. If all goes well, at some point in the future the foreign central bank repays the Fed by replenishing its account. If things go badly, all the Fed has is an account balance at the foreign central bank—a promise to pay foreign currency in a foreign country. FIMA, open to over a hundred counterparties, enters into purchase-and-sale agreements like the ones the Fed conducts with the primary dealers to lend dollars in exchange for collateral in the form of US Treasury securities. If the recipients of FIMA loans do not or cannot pay the Fed back, the Fed is fully secured by US government debt. The FIMA repo facility is open only to foreign central banks that hold their Treasury securities with the Federal Reserve Bank of New York. The program, announced on March 31, received little use. By the time it was operational, foreign shadow banks were much more stable. Usage peaked at $1 billion on May 14.

market champion (and editor-in-chief of *The Economist*) Walter   45
Bagehot, who famously remarked that a panic "is a species of
neuralgia, and according to the rules of science you must not
starve it." What Bagehot meant is that if people believe a firm
issuing money claims might fail, that alone may well be enough
to bring failure about. The solution—at least once the fires start
raging—is to feed the beast: to lend financial firms however
much government cash they need to prove that their money
claims are (and will remain) equivalent.

Nevertheless, despite the Fed's repeating its 2008 playbook
and offering generous lending terms to a wide range of financial
firms, as the week of March 16 ended, the panic was still intensifying. One problem was that several of the announced facilities would not be up and running for days or weeks. Another
was that, despite the Fed's avowed commitments, markets
remained skeptical that all eligible firms would be able to use
the programs.

The trouble was evident in the unprecedented—previously
unimaginable—turmoil in the market for the safest financial
asset in the world: US Treasury securities. Instead of increasing
in value, as Treasury securities nearly universally do when
times are tough and investors are looking for a safe haven, the
price of Treasury securities plunged. The implied cost to the
US government of servicing a ten-year bond rose from 0.54 percent per year to 1.18 percent per year—doubling in a matter of
days. As a result, liquidity in Treasury markets dried up: if you
wanted to sell a Treasury security, the transaction costs you'd
incur were higher than they had ever been before.

Why were Treasuries plummeting in value? Did people
believe that the US government was going to default? No. The

46   drop in the value of Treasury securities was driven by the fact that so many of the financial institutions (and foreign central banks) that owned Treasury securities were facing runs (and runs on their financial sectors); they were thus forced to sell these investments at whatever the price to satisfy their obligations. It was an unheard of form of collateral damage stemming from the fragility of shadow banks.

The Fed was staring down an ever-worsening cycle of deflation and default that, left uninterrupted, might throw tens of millions of Americans out of work. Even using all of the tools from 2008, lending dollars to stumbling financial firms was simply proving too difficult and too slow. So, the Fed decided to try to stop the panic by directly stepping into the void as purchaser, an action it had never before taken to stop a panic. As it started buying US Treasury bonds and mortgage-backed securities, its goal was to support financial firms by buying so many assets that the price would start to rise again. In this way, the Fed would tackle the proximate cause of the panic: the fall in asset prices caused by COVID.

The Fed started these "market functioning purchases" on March 13, at a staggering pace of $30 to $50 billion of securities per day. On March 19, the Fed hit the accelerator, adding over $80 billion in a matter of hours. Over the next six days, the Fed stunned commentators and market participants by purchasing over $100 billion of bonds per day.

These amounts exceeded, by a large margin, any purchases the Fed had ever previously made. During the global financial crisis a decade prior, the Fed bought over $1 trillion of debt. Those purchases, while themselves unprecedented, unfolded over the course of a year-and-a-half, and their primary goal was

CHART 1.3
Federal Reserve Asset Purchases by Day (in billions of US$)

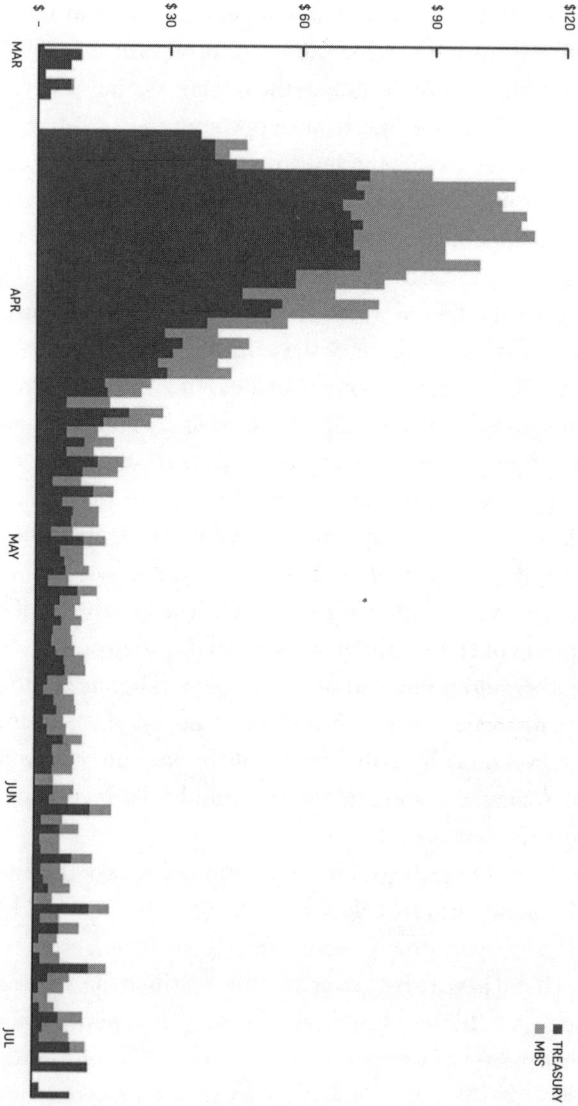

Source: Federal Reserve Bank of New York

TREASURY
MBS

$120

$90

$60

$30

$ -

MAR

APR

MAY

JUN

JUL

48   to strengthen the housing market and help the economy bounce back from the Great Recession—not to stop a panic. But the Fed had learned from 2008: the longer the fire burns, the harder it is to put out and the more dangerous it becomes.

In the middle of this buying spree, on March 26, the Fed's chairman, Jerome Powell, gave a rare TV interview. He promised the American people that the Fed would not "run out of ammunition." What he meant was that there would be no limit to the amount of assets the Fed would be willing to purchase. The Fed would unleash the full power of the printing press.

And within days, the panic subsided. In 2008, the government had showed that it could fight a crisis by lending money to overleveraged financial firms and injecting additional capital through special government investments. In March 2020, the Fed developed a new way to prevent financial catastrophe: by directly buying trillions of dollars of financial assets. Powell's interview seemed to hint at untold possibilities. In theory, if the Fed wanted, could it take the entire financial system onto its balance sheet? Could it buy $20 or $30 trillion of bonds? Could it buy *all the financial assets* in the entire economy? If so, no company need ever default again. That would be one sure way to stabilize the financial system. If the Fed could fully reverse asset price sell-offs, why panic?

As it turned out, the Fed was not required to take the entire financial system onto its balance sheet in 2020. But it did have to signal to everyone that it would keep the printing press running. And it did have to lend over $1 trillion to financial firms and purchase $1.5 trillion of financial assets on the open market— all within a matter of weeks.

Extending the Fed's Embrace

Although the panic was over by late March, the economic out-look for the country remained gloomy for much longer. Unlike in 2008 and 2009, when the economy shrank as a result of financial collapse, economic activity slowed down in 2020 for reasons that had little to do with the financial sector.* Nor were financial firms the only ones facing peril. The rapidly spreading pandemic and accompanying shutdowns threatened the well-being of local businesses, ordinary households, and state and local governments. On March 27, with so much support flowing to Wall Street, Congress decided to lend a hand to Main Street by passing the CARES Act, a massive economic stabilization package that targeted the broader economy.

Most of the relief provided by the CARES Act did not involve the Fed. The law appropriated money for the Small Business Administration to distribute to restaurants, cinemas, and other businesses that were struggling to make payroll. It authorized the IRS to distribute over $1 trillion in cash to households making less than $200,000 per year. And it gave the Treasury Secretary money to support airlines and other critical industries.

But one prong of the CARES Act did involve the Fed. Without amending the Federal Reserve Act, Congress authorized the Fed to extend its embrace beyond the financial sector for the purpose of stabilizing the economy. As we will see, the Fed is not a government credit authority: unlike commercial

* Of course, had the panic continued it would have had its own dire impact on labor markets and business solvency.

50   banks (and even other government agencies), it is not set up to interact with the general public. The Fed's primary lending power is for providing liquidity to banks, to ensure that bank deposits are always interchangeable with cash. And its non-bank lending power is for providing liquidity to shadow banks (and other parts of the financial system) to achieve similar ends with respect to various alternative forms of money. But as the pandemic shut down whole sectors of the economy, Congress wanted the Fed to do more, a desire that at least some officials within the Fed itself shared. The CARES Act made this possible: it enabled the Fed to lend to businesses, nonprofits, and municipalities by providing legal cover and loss-absorbing capacity. Specifically, it appropriated $500 billion for the Treasury Secretary to use to backstop Fed facilities that extend credit to businesses and municipalities, including by buying bonds and other investment instruments on secondary markets.

The first new vehicles off the blocks were two "corporate credit facilities"—the Primary Market Corporate Credit Facility and the Secondary Market Corporate Credit Facility, programs for supporting large corporations and their investors. The Fed announced these programs on March 23, even before the president signed the CARES Act into law. Ultimately, the Treasury said it would backstop them with $75 billion from the CARES Act and the Fed pledged to use its printing press to lend up to $750 billion.

The Primary Corporate Credit Facility targeted debt issued by investment-grade US companies (those in good financial shape prior to the start of the pandemic), which were headquartered in the US and had material operations in the US. The Secondary Facility was created to augment these efforts

TABLE 1.2
The Fed's Bond ETF Holdings (as of January 2021)

HOLDING	AMOUNT IN BILLIONS
High Yield Corporate Bond ETFs	$ 1.16
Investment Grade, Intermediate Term Corporate Bond ETFs	$ 5.09
Investment Grade, Short Term Corporate Bond ETFs	$ 2.53

Source: Federal Reserve Board

by purchasing bonds issued by qualifying companies on the secondary market. The Fed subsequently authorized the Secondary Facility to also purchase exchange-traded bond funds—mutual funds that own portfolios of bonds—including those invested in high-yield (aka "junk") bonds, i.e., debt securities issued by companies in bad financial shape prior to the start of the pandemic.

The Primary Corporate Credit Facility, which was authorized to lend only upon application and charged a 100-basis point (1 percent) facility fee, never ended up making any loans before it was discontinued in December 2020. Since large corporations were able to access credit markets and other Fed policies had helped improve credit spreads significantly, eligible borrowers had little need for this (relatively) costly funding. By contrast, the Fed's Secondary Facility bought over a thousand bonds and sixteen exchange-traded funds at market prices (see Tables 1.2 and 1.3 listing the identities of some of the beneficiaries, which included companies like AT&T, Ford, and Apple). These acquisitions, totaling $13.5 billion, remained on the Fed's books into 2021.

The Secondary Facility also functioned quite differently from the Primary Facility. Since it bought securities on the open

52 market, it did not extend credit *directly* to any borrowers. As the
Fed put it, the Secondary Corporate Credit Facility "support[ed]
credit to employers by providing liquidity to the market for
outstanding corporate bonds." A large point of the Secondary
Market Corporate Credit Facility, in other words, was to lower
the cost and reduce the time for market participants to trade
corporate bonds. Many of the program's immediate beneficiaries were financial firms that bought and sold corporate
bonds and existing owners of corporate bonds, especially those
looking to buy or sell them. In this sense, the Secondary Market
Corporate Credit Facility functioned as another means of supporting shadow banks.

TABLE 1.3
The Fed's Top Ten Corporate Bond Holdings
(as of January 2021)

ISSUER	SECTOR	AMOUNT IN MILLIONS
AT&T Inc	Telecommunications	$ 98
Toyota Motor Credit Corp	Consumer / Financial	$ 96
Daimler Finance North America LLC	Consumer / Financial	$ 93
Verizon Communications Inc	Telecommunications	$ 92
Volkswagen Group of America Finance LLC	Consumer / Financial	$ 90
Apple Inc	Technology	$ 88
Comcast Corp	Communications	$ 85
BMW US Capital LLC	Consumer / Financial	$ 70
General Electric Co	Capital Goods	$ 68
Ford Motor Credit Co LLC	Consumer / Financial	$ 68
Microsoft Corp	Technology	$ 67
AbbVie Inc	Healthcare	$ 58
CVS Health Corp	Healthcare	$ 53
BP Capital Markets America Inc	Energy	$ 53
General Motors Financial Co Inc	Consumer / Financial	$ 50

Source: Federal Reserve Board

On March 23, the Fed also rolled out the Term Asset-Backed
Securities Loan Facility, a program it had first developed in 2008.
TALF 2.0 was slated to lend up to $100 billion to financial and
nonfinancial firms against highly rated, dollar-denominated
securities, in which the underlying credit exposures included
auto loans, student loans, and credit card receivables. Like the
Secondary Market Corporate Credit Facility, TALF 2.0 helped
some alternative money issuers—those that issued commercial paper. But, in line with its stated objective, TALF 2.0 also
increased the flow of credit to end users, like car buyers, by
supporting markets for asset-based securities and therefore
encouraging financial firms to extend credit to consumers.

The next round of programs, announced on April 9, included another program that provided overflow benefits to financial firms: the Municipal Liquidity Facility. The MLF's primary
beneficiaries were local governments. Drawing on a $35 bil-
lion Treasury backstop, the MLF was authorized to purchase
up to $500 billion of short-term debt issued by states, cities
with a population exceeding 1 million residents, and counties
with a population exceeding 2 million residents. On April 27,
the Fed lowered the population threshold to 500,000 for counties and 250,000 for cities and extended eligible duration from
two years to three. And in June, the Fed further modified the
terms to allow more cities and countries in less populous states
to participate in the program.

The Fed has long had the authority to buy short-term debt
issued by state and local governments. However, it has not used
this authority since 1933. One reason for this is that, unlike
debt issued by the federal government, municipal debt sometimes defaults. In 2013, for example, the City of Detroit declared

54   bankruptcy,* and its creditors received between fourteen and
        seventy-five cents on the dollar. Municipal debt is there-
        fore more difficult to price. While credit rating agencies regu-
        larly evaluate the risk of municipal bonds, their ratings become
        significantly less useful during a crisis, and the Fed lacks the
        in-house capacity to conduct its own review.

        A desire to avoid ending up owning troubled municipal debt
        may partly explain why the Municipal Liquidity Facility set such
        high interest rates. Another reason was that the Fed needed the
        Treasury Secretary's sign-off on the terms of the loans and Sec-
        retary Mnuchin may have opposed broader lending that would
        have supported city and state governments. Regardless, by
        the time the MLF was operational, most municipalities were
        already able to access substantially cheaper financing from
        other lenders.** This mismatch, with the Fed offering to lend
        at rates above those generally available in private markets, per-
        sisted for nearly the entire life of the program, which explains
        why the Fed ultimately purchased municipal bonds from only
        two issuers—New York's Metropolitan Transit Authority and
        the State of Illinois.

        Nevertheless, the Municipal Liquidity Facility had a variety
        of significant economic effects. One group of beneficiaries, as
        mentioned earlier, were Wall Street firms. These firms deal in

        * Other recent municipal bankruptcies include Jefferson County, Alabama
        (2011), and Stockton, California (2012).

        ** The MLF included a 10-basis point "origination fee," plus it charged annual
        interest at a rate 100 basis points above the comparable maturity Overnight
        Index Swap rate for municipalities with a AAA rating (the highest) and 330
        basis points for municipalities with BBB- ratings (the lowest rating still
        considered "investment grade").

TABLE 1.4
The Fed's Municipal Loans

BORROWER	DATE	NOTE VALUE IN BILLIONS	INTEREST RATE	DURATION
State of Illinois	6/2/2020	$ 1.20	3.36%	1 Year
State of Illinois	12/14/2020	$ 2.00	3.42%	3 Years
Metropolitan Transportation Authority (NY)	8/18/2020	$ 0.45	1.93%	3 Years
Metropolitan Transportation Authority (NY)	12/9/2020	$ 2.91	1.33%	3 Years

Source: Federal Reserve Board

municipal securities and with the Municipal Liquidity Facility in place they could more easily and confidently make markets (buying from sellers and selling to buyers) knowing that the Fed was willing to serve as a "buyer of last resort." Firms that already held municipal securities also benefited: the price of municipal bonds went up because people became less worried about the possibility that cities would default on their debt, since the Fed would be willing to step in and help state and local governments if conditions deteriorated.

State and local governments, of course, also benefited. Those that needed to issue more debt, either to pay off existing debt or to cover new shortfalls, could borrow in the private markets for lower rates, given the assurance that the Fed's backstop provided to lenders. In other words, many municipalities benefited from the Municipal Liquidity Facility even though the Fed never bought their bonds. Some benefits even reached municipal workers: by and large, state and local governments avoided the mass layoffs that upended lives and crippled the economy in 2008 and 2009.

56   The other CARES Act initiatives targeted medium-sized
enterprises. Six new facilities were for businesses and nonprofits without credit ratings or access to the capital markets:
five known collectively as the Main Street Lending Program,*
and the Paycheck Protection Program Liquidity Facility, which
supported the CARES Act Paycheck Protection Program run by
the Small Business Administration. Unlike the corporate credit
facilities announced in March, these Main Street facilities
were designed to invest in organizations that often lacked the
in-house legal and accounting expertise to apply for and nego-
tiate loan agreements.

The Fed offered Main Street loans—underwritten, originated, and serviced with the help of commercial banks—to US
businesses with up to 15,000 employees or up to $5 billion in
2019 annual revenues (subject to a variety of further limitations, including leverage limits of between four and six times
2019 adjusted earnings). Borrowers were barred from using
the proceeds of these loans to bolster executive compensa-
tion, repurchase stock, or distribute capital, and were required
to attest that they needed financing due to the exigent circumstances presented by the pandemic. The Fed also required the
for-profit banks that originated Main Street loans to retain 5
percent on their own balance sheets as skin-in-the-game—that
is, the banks would stand to lose at least some money if they
underwrote loans that were never paid back. (In cases involving
more leveraged borrowers, the Fed required banks to retain 15

---

* The Main Street New Loan Facility ("MSNLF"), the Main Street Expanded
Loan Facility ("MSELF"), the Main Street Priority Loan Facility ("MSPLF"),
the Nonprofit Organization New Loan Facility ("NONLF"), and the
Nonprofit Organization Expanded Loan Facility ("NOELF").

percent.) To further protect itself, the Fed secured $75 billion from the Treasury's CARES Act appropriation to absorb potential losses from its Main Street Lending Program.

Like the Municipal Liquidity Facility, the Main Street program charged a high interest rate: a 1 percent facility fee and 3 percent spread over LIBOR (the benchmark interest rate at which banks lend to one another). And because the program also required (profit-seeking) banks to retain skin-in-the-game, take-up was relatively limited. Banks did not want to sell their good loans to the Fed. Nor did they want to make new loans that might not be paid back if they were going to have to shoulder some of the losses. The biggest loan, originated by Bank of America, ended up being $300 million to Fitness International LLC, a California company that runs gyms. Other borrowers included energy companies like El Dorado Oil & Gas, a Mississippi outfit that borrowed $50 million; Finley Production, an energy conglomerate with thousands of well sites around the country ($130 million); and Palisades Arcadia Baseball LLC, which owns one of the most storied minor league baseball franchises, the Dayton Dragons. Overall, the Fed purchased around 1,800 loans totaling $16.5 billion, a fraction of the program's $600 billion capacity.*

---

* The Paycheck Protection Program Liquidity Facility operated a bit differently from the other CARES Act programs. The Small Business Administration guarantees PPP loans, which functioned more like conditional grants, so the Fed did not take on any credit risk through the PPPLF. Banks originated and serviced loans, and the Fed's facility bought them from the banks, exchanging the loans for dollars, which the banks could then use to make additional loans. The PPPLF made over 10,000 advances to over 500 banks, totaling around $70 billion, over the same period that the PPP program itself lent over $650 billion.

TABLE 1.5

The Fed's CARES Act Facilities During the Pandemic

DATE	FACILITY	LIMIT	MAXIMUM USAGE	NUMBER OF LOANS
3/23	Term Asset-Backed Securities Loan Facility (TALF)	$100B	$4.4B	224 loans to 20 borrowers through 14 investment managers
3/23	Primary Market Corporate Credit Facility (PMCCF)	$500B	$0	None
3/23	Secondary Market Corporate Credit Facility (SMCCF)	$250B	$13.5B	1,084 bonds from 520 issuers and 16 ETFs
4/9	Municipal Liquidity Facility (MLF)	$500B	$6.3B	2 bonds to Illinois; 2 bonds to New York's Metropolitan Transit Authority
4/9	Main Street Lending Program (MSLP)	$600B	$16.5B	1,810 loans to 1,796 borrowers through 318 lenders
4/9	PPP Loan Facility (PPPLF)	$349B	$72B	>10,000 advances to >500 banks

Source: Federal Reserve Board

The collection of CARES Act programs run by the Fed represented a significant change in Fed policy. The programs involved Fed purchases of corporate and municipal debt, as well as loans to big and medium-sized businesses and nonprofits—activities that, as we shall soon see, are quite different from the Fed's traditional role as a monetary authority charged with ensuring that money created by the banking system trades at par with government cash. The Fed's credit programs allocated capital directly, as in the case of the Main Street program, or indirectly, by enhancing liquidity in secondary markets. These programs put the Fed in the role of a crisis-times "national investment authority," employing its balance sheet in ways that shape economic activity. Normally, this is the kind of activity that banks

perform for profit. During the pandemic, the Fed was enlisted
by Congress to do it in the public interest.

QE Infinity

There is another dimension of the Fed's response to the pandemic that bears mentioning. As the panic subsided, the Fed continued its purchases of government debt. Its goal ceased being to absorb selling pressure from financial firms and foreign central banks; that pressure had dissipated. Instead, the Fed wanted to lower interest rates for long-term borrowing below where they had been prior to the pandemic, thereby stimulating economic activity. The press labeled the initiative QE Infinity. It involved $120 billion of purchases per month ($80 billion of Treasury securities and $40 billion in MBS).

QE Infinity has had several effects. First, it has increased the price of financial and nonfinancial assets. By buying bonds for its own books, the Fed has raised the price of bonds and lowered their yields (the returns that investors receive when they buy bonds at current market prices and hold them to maturity). Indirectly, the Fed's bond buying has also raised the price of stocks, both by providing bond investors with cash that some of them redeploy into stocks, and by lowering the Discount Rate that investors apply to companies' projected cash flows when valuing their equity securities. And as the value of stocks and bonds has gone up, the value of other assets, such as real estate, has followed, in part because as bond yields fall, mortgage rates tend to fall (making it easier to finance real estate purchases), and in part because people who buy assets like real estate tend to own financial assets, and as

60   the value of their financial assets increases, they are able to pay more for real estate.

Second, QE Infinity has lowered the cost of servicing debt. As debt service costs go down, people carrying high debt loads are able to keep making their payments even if their earnings drop. Low interest rates also mean that companies may be able to borrow more money to invest in new projects, stimulating employment and production.

Third, by buying mortgage bonds in particular, the Fed has directly stimulated real estate prices. The more money a household can borrow at any given level of monthly mortgage payment, the more it can afford to pay for a home. When everyone's borrowing capacity expands at the same time, and the housing stock stays roughly the same, home prices rise.

Through these different channels, the Fed was able to address economic stagnation even after it had lowered overnight borrowing rates for banks to between 0 and 0.25 percent, a range known as the "zero-lower bound." With rates at the zero-lower bound, there was not much more the Fed could do using conventional means to induce banks to make new loans. QE Infinity, therefore, gave the Fed a way to respond to high unemployment without taking more drastic steps to stimulate banks to expand their balance sheets (such as adjusting supervisory or regulatory policies). And unlike most other government initiatives that involve outlays of money, QE Infinity did not take an act of Congress. Nor did the program drive up the national debt, because the Fed financed it with newly created money.

Cui Bono?[*]   61

The Fed's pandemic response—including its panic-fighting actions, CARES Act lending programs, and QE Infinity—has been widely hailed, and for good reason. The Fed used the tools at its disposal to reduce financial and economic disruption. Where it crossed "red lines," acting in ways it never had before, it did so with congressional backing and in favor of greater action, not less. Action in a crisis is usually better than inaction. As Tim Geithner, one of the leading architects of the federal government's response to the 2008 collapse, put it, "Plan beats no plan." By preventing another Great Recession, or possibly Great Depression, the Fed provided significant, broad-based benefits to society.

Yet just as not everyone benefits equally from a tax cut, or a government program like Medicaid, not everyone benefited equally from the Fed's response to the pandemic. Plan might beat no plan, but some plans are better than others. The inconvenient truth is that the Fed's policy cocktail greatly assisted the already well-off, skewing benefits toward the richest Americans and driving wealth inequality to levels not seen since before the New Deal. To appreciate the disparities experienced by different beneficiaries of the Fed's response, consider two hypothetical examples.

First, imagine two families of four: the Debtmans and Asseters. The Debtmans rent an apartment for $2,000 per month. The father, Derrick, works in hospitality: he's a waiter at a local restaurant, where he earns $8 per hour plus tips. On a good Friday or Saturday night he nets several hundred dollars. The

[*] Latin for "to whom is it a benefit?" or simply "who benefits?"

62   mother, Delia, works at a retail pharmacy chain. Delia has good healthcare: her employer covers her whole family. And she earns $15 per hour now, the result of a new minimum wage law her state recently adopted. Most years, Derrick and Delia take home $80,000 between them—a comfortable sum. But the Debtmans still live paycheck to paycheck. Although their kids attend public high schools, the Debtmans have accumulated $25,000 in credit card debt to cover the costs of soccer practice, guitar lessons, and summer camp.

The Asseters live in a major city center. They also have $20,000 of credit card debt—childcare for their two daughters, ages three and seven, is not cheap. But years ago, they inherited some money from their grandparents, which they used for a down payment: they own their apartment, paying around $2,000 per month in interest and principal on their $400,000 mortgage. The Asseters work full-time: Amelia is a professor at a university making $100,000 per year; Alex is a social worker at a nearby hospital, earning $60,000 annually, with generous benefits. Unlike the Debtmans, the Asseters have some savings: their employers pay 5 percent of their salary every year into a 401(k) retirement plan. Together, they've built a nest egg— $500,000, which they have invested in a balanced portfolio of stocks and bonds.

A year into the pandemic, both families are doing better than they might have expected when the virus first struck. As part of a pharmacy chain, Delia was an essential worker and so kept earning a paycheck. As a waiter, Derrick was furloughed for a few months. But the federal unemployment program fully covered his lost wages, and now he is back at work. Financially,

the Debtmans are no worse off. Maybe they are even doing a 63
bit better: the kids are spending more time at home, which has
allowed Delia and Derrick to pay down a few thousand dollars of
their credit card debt.

Alex and Amelia, meanwhile, are also relieved to have made
it through what they hope was the worst of the crisis. With
Alex working long hours in a high-risk environment at the hospital, and Amelia struggling to find childcare, it's been a difficult
year. Amelia and Alex ran up their credit card debt a bit—
their kids' school went hybrid, which required them to hire a
lot more help at home. But they aren't worried. The adjustable
rate on their mortgage dropped 40 basis points, saving them
hundreds of dollars a month. Last month, when the Asseters
checked their savings, they were surprised to see that their balance had jumped 25 percent since February 2020: their 401(k)
now topped $625,000. Later, while poking around on Zillow,
Amelia discovered that homes in their area were selling for 15
percent more than last year. The Asseters' most valuable asset
had always been their home: since they bought it in 2010 for
$450,000, it had doubled in value. Now it was worth over $1
million. And Zillow estimated that the value had increased a full
$125,000 since early 2020. The Asseters did the math, and they
were shocked: they made more money in the past year on their
investments—their apartment and their savings—than from
their jobs.

A similar sort of dynamic played out among businesses.
Consider two firms. One is a blue-chip American mainstay: its
stock is traded on the New York Stock Exchange, and it regu-
larly raises cash in the bond market to finance its operations.

64   Before the pandemic, it paid around 3.8 percent on its debt, which accounted for about half of its enterprise value. The other is a well-established local concern. It employs 2,000 people and relies on small amounts of bank credit to make payroll and smooth its cash flows. Debt has never been a big part of its business model: the company's owners, several related families, some of whom are still involved in running things, try to keep it well capitalized and draw modest annual dividends.

Both companies make widgets—let's keep it simple—and the market for widgets held up pretty well during the pandemic. Sales for both fell during the initial shutdown but spiked in the second half of the year, leaving net revenue about where everyone thought it would be in January. Nonetheless, profits for both companies are up. The local stalwart received a Main Street Loan, which it was able to use to cover the shortfall in the first half of the year. By year end, credit markets were so strong that it was able to refinance some of its existing debt. The blue-chip company was *really* flourishing. Over the summer, the Fed's Corporate Credit Facility purchased $50 million of the company's bonds on the open market. Overall, it saw its interest expense—the annual bill it pays on its debt—drop from 3.8 percent to 3.2 percent. Never in its history had it been able to borrow so cheaply. As a result, the company had substantially more money left over at the end of the year for dividends.

The Fed's programs played a major role in shaping these outcomes. First, by stopping the panic, the Fed averted a credit crunch that would have caused millions of people to lose their jobs and could easily have meant a pay cut for Alex and Amelia or put Derrick and Delia out of work. Second, by lowering interest rates and launching QE Infinity, the Fed hastened the recovery:

bringing Derrick back to his restaurant sooner, helping Amelia's
university keep tuition money rolling in, and making it easier
for Delia's pharmacy chain to keep the lights on. Yet while the
Fed's programs helped both couples, Alex and Amelia came out
ahead—*way ahead*—of Derrick and Delia. Because the former
owned assets, the Fed's efforts translated into a wealth increase
of hundreds of thousands of dollars.

Something similar happened with the local stalwart and
the blue-chip company. For both, the Fed's response was vital.
They were able to keep operating, people kept buying their widgets, and they were able to make payroll. But for the blue chip,
the pandemic brought higher than expected profits. Debt costs
dropped so much as a result of the Fed's asset purchases that
the shareholders saw a windfall. Meanwhile, for the local stalwart, little changed: the Fed kept things together and that meant
business as usual.

Perhaps the biggest winners in 2020 were the wealthiest 0.1
percent of households.* The billionaire class saw its share of the
national income skyrocket. Jeff Bezos went from being worth an
estimated $114 billion in October 2019—a few months before
the pandemic hit—to an astounding $201 billion by October
2021. Elon Musk's fortune increased from $20 billion to $190
billion over the same period—a 600 percent gain. The founder
of Nike, Phil Knight, saw his wealth almost double (from $36

---

* Two groups took wealth share during the pandemic: the top 1 percent, which
gained 2.21 percentage points (reaching 32.07 percent of household net
worth), and the bottom 50 percent, which generally do not own assets, but
due to fiscal transfer payments and the Fed's low interest rate policies were
able to pay down debts, gaining almost one-fifth of one percentage point
(reaching 2.02 percent of household net worth).

66   billion to $60 billion), as did the founders of Google (Larry Page and Sergey Brin), Facebook (Mark Zuckerberg), and Oracle (Larry Ellison). Between March 18, 2020—when the Fed hit the gas and markets began to recover from their nadir—and August of 2021, US billionaires collectively saw their wealth increase from $2.95 trillion to over $4.7 trillion, a roughly 60 percent gain, substantially higher than the pace of economic growth over the same period.

Of course, paper gains for the richest Americans should not deter the government from pursuing policies that improve the prospects of ordinary households and businesses. Nor is Fed policy alone responsible for this jump in the largest fortunes. Interest rates (the cost of borrowing money) are bound to fall in an environment, like a pandemic, where more and more people are living for tomorrow. And when interest rates fall, assets are easier to buy today, and the value of future cash flows rises. This disproportionately enriches the already rich. The pandemic also accelerated other economic trends (such as consolidation and the rise of e-commerce) that buttressed the value of many large companies. But given the role that the Fed did play in altering the price of assets, people are now wondering whether the Fed could and should adjust its approach and use its balance sheet to combat climate change, finance state and local governments, or relieve the burdens of ordinary debtors. In other words, is there some way for the Fed to tackle macroeconomic management—a major undertaking that the Fed was never expected to handle on its own—in a way that distributes wealth in a more equitable manner?

To determine whether the Fed is likely to be able to execute such a task, and to appreciate just how much the Fed's activities have expanded in the past fourteen years, we must go back and figure out why Congress established the Fed in the first place and how the Fed is designed to work. We must examine the way that money is created in America, and see why the rise of new moneymakers has transformed the Fed and turned the world upside down.

Money and Banking in America

A defining feature of the American economy, from the turn of the nineteenth century to the present day, is that it relies on investor-owned banks to create the vast majority of the money that people use. For the government to delegate this sort of power to private shareholders is no small matter, and for most of

US National Bank Note issued by
The Flat Top National Bank of Bluefield in 1929.

American history it was a source of continuous political contro- 69
versy. In the 1790s, Alexander Hamilton and Thomas Jefferson
battled over an investor-owned corporation that Congress
chartered to issue money: the Bank of the United States. In the
1830s, Andrew Jackson waged war on its successor. In the 1870s,
1880s, and 1890s, a series of third-party movements chal-
lenged Democrats and Republicans on platforms of replacing
bank-issued money with government-issued money. Proponents of investor-owned banks argued that the profit motive
was indispensable: if the government issued the whole money
supply, politicians would inevitably fall prey to the temptation
to create too much money and the country's economy would
eventually stagnate. Opponents saw the government's recruit-
ment of shareholder-appointed executives to issue the money
supply as damaging to democracy. To them, for-profit banks
were bastions of privilege, a cancer on the body politic, and a
source of monopoly profits.

US Legal Tender Note ("Greenback")
issued by the US Treasury Department in 1861.

70   Between the Civil War and the Great Depression, American political elites arrived at a compromise: they paired monetary outsourcing with a series of safeguards. I call the institutional ordering that emerged the American Monetary Settlement. One of the centerpieces of the settlement is the Federal Reserve, which Congress established in 1913 and refined in 1935. The Fed is built to channel the efforts of privately owned banks toward public ends, thereby preserving the investor-owned banking system and rebuffing efforts to replace bank money with government-issued currency. To understand how the Fed is supposed to do this, this chapter unpacks the American Monetary Settlement and the reasons that legislators developed the key features of US banking law.

The English Arrangement

As with many foundational elements of the American state, the idea of using banks to expand the money supply came from England. There, beginning in the 1690s, Parliament, the Crown, and London's business elites worked out an unprecedented monetary arrangement. Parliament agreed to fix the amount of gold and silver bullion in the money it issued, coins known as pounds, and pledged not to alter this amount or to issue pounds without backing them with gold or silver (no paper notes, for example). To expand the money supply so that the economy could grow, Parliament chartered an investor-owned corporation, the Bank of England, which it empowered to issue paper notes and maintain account entries known as deposits. Together, these forms of "bank money" supplemented a base of government-issued gold and silver coins. Although the Bank of England promised to pay coins in exchange for its notes and

deposits, people treated the Bank's notes and deposits as money   71
primarily because they were convenient, and people were confident that the government stood behind the enterprise.

This new approach to money was not without its drawbacks. To limit the Bank's power and prevent it from monopo-
lizing various markets and trades, Parliament prohibited it from
engaging in commercial activities. And to bolster the Bank's
financial position and to prevent competing entities from
undermining confidence in the Bank's notes and deposits, Parliament pledged not to charter any other banks. It also prohibited partnerships and corporations within sixty-five miles of
London from circulating paper notes as money.

In the 1790s, at the suggestion of Alexander Hamilton, then
Secretary of the Treasury, Congress set up a similar system in
the United States. Congress fixed the price of dollars in terms of
gold and silver and pledged not to issue dollars without backing
them with the requisite amount of gold or silver. To expand the
supply of dollars, Congress chartered the Bank of the United
States, a federal corporation controlled by private shareholders.
Congress prohibited the Bank of the United States from engaging
in other lines of business and promised it that federal legislators would not charter any other banks. States set up parallel
institutions like the Bank of New York and the Massachusetts
Bank, which were subject to similar restrictions and authorized
to expand the money supply in their jurisdictions within limits
set informally by the Bank of the United States.

The American Monetary Settlement

But the English monetary system did not take to American soil.
There were two problems. First, the owners and managers of the

72 Bank of the United States looked like a new aristocracy. As one writer put it in 1819: "The [C]ongress of the United States, by the charter of the [Bank of the United States], has lost the power to control its concerns in their most essential particulars." By allowing private investors to expand the money supply, the government had lodged "vast power . . . in the hands of less than fifty individuals, who may make the whole monied capital of the United States bow to them, or suffer incalculable derangements and losses." To the Bank's critics, this was "an aristocracy worthy of the resistance . . . an aristocracy paramount to the law of the United States."

Second, the new bankers were mostly from a single political party: the Federalists. This attempt at partisan entrenchment proved fatal. While Hamilton and others anticipated sustained opposition to banking from agrarian political leaders like Thomas Jefferson, they did not foresee the emergence of the two-party system and the subsequent movement by Jefferson's party to charter "Republican" banks to compete with the Bank of the United States and its state cousins. As Jefferson's party took control of state governments and the number of state banks grew, so did resentment of the Bank and its dominant position. In the 1830s, the political foundations of the system collapsed. President Andrew Jackson vetoed a bill to renew the Bank's charter and drove its executives out of power.

Over the next forty years, the American Monetary Settlement took shape. The state legislators who initially developed its key aspects agreed with the founding generation that the power to expand the money supply was too great to be left in the hands of elected bodies. Affording politicians this power would lead to corruption, stagnation, and a debased currency. But they were also afraid to concentrate the power in the hands of a few unelected executives. So, they attempted to steer a middle course by diffusing the power across different entities and constraining it as much as possible. They set up a system of chartered banks whereby anyone willing and able to comply with certain terms and conditions could apply for permission to create money.

In 1864, Congress federalized this arrangement by passing the National Bank Act. It did so, in part, to head off demands that the government continue to issue greenbacks, paper money created by the government to pay for the Civil War. The Act instead created a bureau in the Treasury Department to charter "national banks." National banks, which remain the backbone of our monetary system, expand the money supply so the government does not have to. Congress expected that national banks would replace the patchwork of state banks. To that end, it granted national banks an effective monopoly on paper money creation by taxing all other notes out of existence.

The American Monetary Settlement has four central components. First, as we've already seen, delegation—government-chartered banks,* rather than the government itself, are primarily responsible for expanding the money supply. Second, separation—chartered banks are barred from engaging in commercial activities, and thus from competing with the people to

---

* In addition to national banks and state-chartered banks, the US also employs several types of special purpose depository institutions including savings and loan associations and credit unions. This book uses the term *bank* to refer to all government-chartered depository institutions.

74   whom they lend. Third, diffusion—the power to issue money is spread out across many banks so that charters are available on a nonpartisan basis and every community can have its own banks. And fourth, supervision—special government officials use broad oversight powers to ensure that banks operate in the public interest and that the money they issue is "safe and sound."

US legislators derived pillars one and two—delegation and separation—from the English arrangement discussed above. Pillars three and four—diffusion and supervision—are American innovations designed to make delegation politically viable. Diffusion and supervision go together: placing the power to create money in a multitude of private hands, rather than just a few, was a radical idea that required a distinct mode of governance, one that is informal, technocratic, and discretionary. Let's now look more closely at each of these pillars. The Fed, as we will see in the next chapter, is an extension of pillar four.

Pillar One: Delegation

Delegation is where any attempt to understand the Fed must begin. It is the foundation of the modern Anglo-American monetary order. The United States has used investor-owned banks to expand the money supply since the 1790s. As mentioned, the money these banks issue takes the form of either notes or deposits. Notes are printed and can be passed from hand to hand. Deposits are entries in a spreadsheet or ledger book. But they are quite similar to each other: a note is a "certificated" deposit, i.e., a deposit in physical form that can be transferred more easily. Today, only the twelve Federal Reserve Banks

issue notes.* But deposits, which can be used to make payments by paper check or electronic wire, are the primary monetary instruments, in our society. Only chartered banks issue
deposits.

One instance in which banks create deposits is when
someone gives them physical cash issued by the government,
for instance, when you take coins to the bank or enter paper
notes into an ATM. In such cases, the bank does not hold this
cash on your behalf to be redeemed at a later date. (As mentioned, a deposit is not like a coat check at a restaurant.) The
bank credits your account, increasing your available balance.
Instead of holding money issued by the government, you now
hold money issued by the bank.

The creation of new deposits does not, however, require that
people trade in government cash. Indeed, most deposits are created as a result of bank lending. The way it works is fairly simple,
if poorly understood. Imagine someone who opens an account
and deposits $1,000 with a teller. Now imagine that person
decides they need $250,000 to buy a new house. Their existing
balance is not nearly enough, so they go to the bank and ask for
a loan. After taking a look at the house, and asking for informa-
tion about the person's income, the bank may decide to extend
the loan. When it does, it simply enters a new number in the person's account: at a keystroke, the balance increases from $1,000

---

* Prior to the Fed's creation, for hand-to-hand payments people used paper
notes issued by publicly chartered, privately owned banks and, for a few
decades in the nineteenth century, paper notes issued by the US Treasury
Department. People also used metal coins issued by the US Mint, which was
established in 1792.

76   to $251,000. The bank does not need cash in the vault to per-
form this action. It just needs a charter from the government.

      This sort of lending—lending in the form of deposits—is
how the supply of money in the economy expands. Government
cash grows only when people want to withdraw cash from the
bank, but deposits grow when people want to borrow to buy a
house, start a business, or build a factory. As a result, there is
roughly $1 trillion of government-issued cash circulating in the
US economy today, most of it in people's wallets, while banks in
the US maintain nearly $18 trillion of deposit account balances.

      Given the relative amounts of cash and deposits in circu-
lation, as well as the much greater volume of transactions that
use deposits (either via check, ACH, or wire), deposits are much
more important than cash when it comes to inflation, employment, and economic growth. An expanding supply of deposits
generally means more jobs and faster growth; a shrinking
volume threatens belt-tightening, defaults, and layoffs. When
the system is working properly, if the economy needs more
money to expand, banks increase their lending: they issue new
deposits. If there are more deposits and cash circulating than
necessary to keep all the country's resources productively
employed, banks reduce the amount of deposits in the economy
by decreasing their lending. (If banks fail to do this, we may
experience inflation: the price of goods and services rises.)

      Banks, of course, cannot create deposits without limit. For
example, banks are constrained by the willingness of people to
use deposits. Before the government put in place measures like
deposit insurance, people were often skeptical of the idea of using
deposits, which might become worthless if the economy hit the
rocks and the bank collapsed. Banks are also constrained by what

economists call "clearing drains"—if one bank starts expanding its balance sheet more quickly than other banks, it will find that its depositors send more transfers to customers of other banks than customers of other banks send to its depositors. When this happens, banks have to reduce their lending or borrow from other banks with excess deposits. And, perhaps most importantly, banks are limited by regulations governing the banking franchise. While banks are empowered to decide who gets to borrow money, government rules incentivize banks to lend to certain borrowers, such as homeowners and governments, cap the aggregate amount of money banks can issue, and require banks to treat low income and minority communities fairly.

Delegating to banks the power to expand the money supply is a policy choice. It limits the role of the government in the economy and restrains the power of political majorities to shape productive activities and distribute private resource endowments. Historically, proponents of delegation have argued that delegation is necessary to prevent inflation. Government officials like Treasury Secretary Alexander Hamilton and Senator John Sherman argued that if the government issued money directly, legislators would be tempted to issue too much. Only by recruiting people motivated by profit, the thinking went, could the state expand the money supply beyond gold and silver without undermining confidence in the currency.*

* Although some people argued that a fully private monetary system was best, with financial firms freely issuing their own paper currencies, most recognized that only a powerful central authority like a state can generate a unit of measurement like the dollar in which a community can value goods and services and that only a state can create a framework in which the money issued by private actors will be accepted by people in both good times and bad.

78   Closely related to the concern about inflation was the fear of expropriation. A government that expands the money supply directly might be tempted to depreciate the currency, thereby expropriating wealth without levying taxes. The present-day insulation of the monetary system from democratic politics, on this view, is not a bug; it is a feature—perhaps the most desirable feature—of a privately owned banking system.

A third factor, less relevant today, was the state's need to cultivate powerful stakeholders. Monetary outsourcing took root and deepened in moments of state formation: in the 1690s, following the Glorious Revolution; in the 1780s and 1790s, following the American Revolution; and in the 1860s, during the Civil War. At each of these junctures, the state sought buy-in from wealthy citizens. By sharing a piece of its power—one that allows a say in economic governance and generates a steady stream of rents—the state gave them a reason to support it. (Of course, these bargains often outlast the wars and exigencies that prompt states to enter into them.)

A fourth argument in favor of delegation concerned corruption. When the federal government established the national banking system during the Civil War, policymakers worried that it would be impossible for the Treasury, once the war had ended, to provide money "in sufficient amounts for the wants of the people" merely by spending it to pay the government's bills. Rather, legislators reasoned, the government would on occasion have to lend money into circulation, which would "convert the treasury into a government bank, with all its hazards and mischiefs." "No Government," one leading congressman explained, "can perform the functions of a bank by loaning money without becoming corrupt and progressively arbitrary and despotic."

Pillar Two: Separation

The second pillar of our banking laws—separation—is as old as delegation itself. As with diffusion and supervision, it was designed to preserve monetary outsourcing by making it politically palatable and institutionally durable. And as with delegation, it dates to the 1690s, when Parliament chartered the Bank of England.

The animating idea behind separation is that banks, which are basically quasi-state enterprises, should be prohibited from engaging in the commercial sphere. The extent to which this ideal should be realized in the American banking system has been a frequent site of disagreement throughout the past century. During the Great Depression, Congress prohibited banks and bank owners from indirectly participating in commerce by, for example, affiliating with securities firms (these laws are popularly referred to as "Glass-Steagall"). Congress also barred *nonbanks* from engaging in banking indirectly by issuing deposits without a banking charter. In 1956, to close further loopholes, Congress passed the Bank Holding Company Act, which it then amended in 1966 and 1970 to prevent evasion. Although regulators and courts repeatedly weakened these separations beginning in the 1980s, Congress has loosened them significantly only once: in 1999, it partially walked back Glass-Steagall by authorizing "Financial Holding Companies" to affiliate banks, securities dealers, and insurers under a single corporate umbrella.

The original reason for separation was to prevent unfair trade practices and limit undue concentrations of private power. Parliament barred the Bank of England from the "buying or selling of any goods, wares, or merchandizes" because it did not

80   want the Bank to "oppress" the merchants and businessmen the Bank was designed to assist. Given the more general aim of the people who forged modern English monetary arrangements—they were trying to protect commercial freedom from an extractive and arbitrary executive—this worry is unsurprising. Unless the Bank was prohibited from entering the commercial sphere, the solution may have proven worse than the problem it was meant to address.

In 1787, Pennsylvania copied Parliament's language almost verbatim in the charter of America's first bank. Similar concerns motivated separation provisions in the 1790s, 1810s, 1830s, and at each of the critical moments when current law was enacted: 1863, 1933, 1956, and 1966. As Congressman William Bourke Cockran put it in 1895, bank money "is not issued for the benefit of the banks, but principally for the benefit of the depositors. Banks cannot absorb all the profits of industry. *They are the servants, not the masters of commerce.*"

Congress also designed statutory limits on bank activities as a means of limiting the power and influence of the people who run banks. The goal here was not to protect commercial liberty, but political liberty. This concern—the possibility that private power could corrupt representative government—motivated US legislators from the battles over the Bank of the United States in the 1790s to the debates about the 1966 amendments to the Bank Holding Company Act. It is also reflected in current law, which authorizes the Fed to block acquisitions of bank shares when it is necessary to prevent not only "decreased or unfair competition" or "conflicts of interest," but also "undue concentration of resources."

Pillar Three: Diffusion

Yet separation was not enough to sustain delegation in the United States. Following a tumultuous period of experimentation that nearly ended in disunion, Congress adopted an approach pioneered in New York and implemented successfully in over a dozen states: diffusion. Congress radically expanded eligibility to open national banks—anyone could apply for a charter—and created a special bureau in the Treasury Department, the Office of the Comptroller of the Currency, to process applications. Diffusion eliminated the special privileges associated with legislative chartering. It also placed the banking power into many hands. To maintain this arrangement over time, legislators also restricted conglomeration. For most of US history and in most states, this meant no branching—banks were limited to one location. Even after Congress relaxed these restrictions in 1927, interstate banking was limited. While Congress dropped its limits in the 1990s, leading to the emergence of large, complex banking organizations, the US banking system remains the most diffuse in the world.

Today, policymakers take for granted the fact that lots of banks compete with each other for customers. But this system, which many other countries have since adopted, was a major innovation when it was introduced. Indeed, some viewed it as irresponsible, given how competition weakens banks, increases the chances of bank failure, and undermines the stability of the monetary system.

The initial impetus for diffusion in the US was to democratize money creation. A political movement, which brought Andrew Jackson to the White House and ultimately threatened to splinter the Democratic Party, successfully argued that money

82 creation should not be a privilege reserved for a select few, but freely available to all. "It is but justice and good policy," President Jackson explained in his message vetoing the recharter of the Bank of the United States, to "let each in his turn enjoy an opportunity to profit by our bounty."

Diffusion was also designed to create a system in which no one bank enjoyed too much stature and importance. As Franklin Roosevelt explained a century later, in calling on Congress to prevent banks from conglomerating through holding company structures, "the liberty of a democracy is not safe if the people tolerate the growth of private power to a point where it becomes stronger than their democratic state itself." In a system with one dominant bank, like the Bank of the United States, even the government may find itself in a subservient position. In a system with many banks, by contrast, each bank checks the others, disciplining overissue and other abuses. A system with multiple banks also gives people a choice about which bank's money to use and opens new avenues to access bank credit.

Diffusion has a further benefit. In a system where banks are small and numerous, bankers are also local. The Bank of the United States, which haunted American policymakers well into the twentieth century, was a distant and alien power to most Americans. Until relatively recently, US banking law created a system in which bankers tended to live in the communities where they banked, which likely enhanced their legitimacy and also may have helped their communities prevent them from abusing their power. To quote President Roosevelt again: private "power [over banking resources] becomes particularly dangerous when it is exercised from a distance."

Pillar Four: Supervision

Diffusion necessitated a further innovation: a new form of technocratic administration to manage a competitive, heterogenous monetary system. With the government no longer handpicking bankers, and with so many bankers spread across the country, the government realized it had to coordinate the activities of the different actors so that the pieces worked together and in the public interest. Long known as "supervision," this mode of governance proceeds through iterative, ongoing, firm-specific engagement. First developed by New York and Massachusetts in the 1830s and 1840s, supervision was incorporated by Congress during the Civil War as part of the National Bank Act. Congress enhanced federal supervision in the 1930s and reinforced it at least once a decade beginning in the 1960s, granting government agencies capacious powers over banks. Today, special government officials write regulatory rules, ensure macroprudential stability, and limit the government's financial exposure to bank balance sheets. Through stress testing and continuous examinations, they ensure that bankers are hewing to their public purposes, rather than taking advantage of their monetary privileges to extract rents.[*]

---

[*] Contemporary supervision stems from the government's power to discipline banks not only when bankers break express legal rules, but whenever, "in the opinion of [the agencies]," bankers are engaging in, have engaged in, or, in the agencies' view, are reasonably believed to be about to engage in "unsafe or unsound practice[s]." Supervisors in the Treasury Department's bureau for national banks, at the Fed, and at the Federal Deposit Insurance Corporation conduct an ongoing dialogue with banks—sharing their concerns about safety and soundness through routine communications and confidential letters—and resolve nearly all issues in private, outside of court.

84   Like diffusion, supervision mitigates concerns about overmighty citizens. Supervisors limit banker discretion and uncover abuses. When faced with instability or scandal in the banking system, Congress has invariably responded by both blaming supervisors and enhancing their power. Indeed, expanding supervisory control, by creating new tools of monetary administration and new ways of directing bank activities, was the impetus for the Federal Reserve Act and the overriding purpose of the Federal Reserve System.

The US monetary system—with investor-owned banks at its center—has long been designed to diffuse power among and between many different actors. Above all, federal legislators attempted to strike a balance between empowering public officials and empowering shareholder-appointed bank executives. This is why they prohibited banks from competing with the businesses they served, restricted their ability to conglomerate, and subjected them to searching oversight by special government supervisors. As we will see in the next chapter, Congress finally created the Fed in 1913 to restrike this balance so as to better ensure that banks benefit the public.

The Logic and Limits of the Federal Reserve Act

By the time Congress created the Fed, the American Monetary Settlement was nearly eighty years old. Thousands of privately owned banks—chartered by the government, separated from commercial enterprises, controlled by local executives, and subject to close oversight by special state and federal officials—issued most of the money in the United States. Yet the settlement remained contested and unstable. For a period in the 1870s it looked like a single, workable legal regime might emerge. But as bank deposits displaced bank notes as the primary monetary instrument, state banking, which had been nearly eliminated by Congress through a tax on state bank notes, returned with a vengeance. Since state banks were not subject to the regulations that Congress crafted in the National Bank Act, their return prompted a "competition in laxity" between state and federal authorities.

Moreover, with banks, both state and federal, operating for profit, no bank had an incentive to look out for the overall performance or stability of the system. Moments of economic

86   uncertainty, when people lost confidence in the value of bank
      assets, triggered monetary contractions and economic depres-
      sions. During these periods, Americans were exposed to the
      power of privately appointed bankers located in cities like New
      York and Chicago, who effectively controlled the money supply.
      With each passing year, these city banks became stronger,
      leaving southern and western regions starved for money and
      credit, especially during downturns. Limited in their regulatory
      tools, government supervisors were unable to mount a mean-
      ingful response. Meanwhile, grassroots movements agitated for
      the government to issue more currency, unwilling to accept the
      role that privately owned banks played in economic life.

      Congress designed the Federal Reserve Act to respond to
      each of these challenges: (1) deflation, (2) maldistribution, and
      (3) insufficient political legitimacy. Although it is common to
      speak of the Fed in the singular, it is best understood as a set of
      multiple institutions working together. It is a *system*: the Federal
      Reserve System. Thousands of banks, called "member banks,"
      make up the foundation. National banks—created by the federal
      government under the National Bank Act—are required to join
      the system. State-chartered banks are given the option to join,
      but the Fed's architects expected that they all would sign up.

      Those who do join must invest in one of the system's twelve
      "Federal Reserve Banks," which are headquartered in twelve dif-
      ferent cities and oversee twelve separate regions of the country.
      Each Federal Reserve Bank is a federally chartered corpora-
      tion, with limited powers and an unusual governance structure
      spelled out in the Federal Reserve Act. Nominally, the member
      banks own the Federal Reserve Banks: they hold all the shares
      and are entitled to a periodic dividend. But they do not control

the Federal Reserve Banks. Instead, they share governance rights
with the centerpiece of the Federal Reserve System: the Federal
Reserve Board (now called the Board of Governors of the Federal Reserve System). The Board of Governors is a government
agency whose job it is to oversee the Federal Reserve Banks, the
member banks, and the rest of the banking system. Each Federal Reserve Bank has its own board of directors, like any corporation, and each is led by its own chief executive officer, or
president. The Board of Governors appoints three of the nine
directors to each Federal Reserve Bank board (including the
chairperson); member banks appoint the other six, three from
among their own number and three from among the community (persons without any ties to the banking system). Together,
the three directors appointed by the Board of Governors and
the three directors selected by the banks from the community
choose a president, whose appointment must also be approved
by the Board of Governors.

The president of the United States, by and within the advice
and consent of the US Senate, appoints the seven governors of
the Board. These governors enjoy fourteen-year terms and can
be removed from office only "for cause" (or via impeachment in
the House and conviction in the Senate). The president may also
nominate one governor to serve as chair, for a term of four years,
subject to Senate confirmation. This gives rise to the Board's
administrative independence: its leaders do not serve at the plea-
sure of the president, nor of any other executive branch official.

Although Congress empowered the Board, in conjunction
with the Reserve Banks, to issue paper currency, legislators did
not want to do away with monetary outsourcing, the arrangement whereby privately owned banks supply most of the money

88   in our society. Congress thus barred the Fed from offering deposit accounts to ordinary people or lending cash to them, leaving privately owned banks to provide this more important form of money and to expand the supply of it by extending credit to households and businesses. Legislators were also careful to prevent the Fed from swallowing their own fiscal powers—the power to tax and spend on behalf of the government—so legislators gave the Fed the power to issue money for a limited purpose: to administer the banking system.

Current law reflects three overarching purposes, each connected with one of the challenges just mentioned: (1) maintaining maximum employment by sustaining monetary expansion over time (accordingly preventing deflation); (2) ensuring a level playing field in the privately managed banking system (thus combating maldistribution); and (3) enhancing public accountability and control over monetary conditions (thereby generating political legitimacy).

Goal One: Monetary Expansion

The most significant pathology in the banking system is its tendency to issue too little money. When the government created banks to expand the money supply and delegated day-to-day control over the banks to privately owned shareholders and their appointed executives, policymakers hoped to avoid politically motivated overissue, i.e., inflation. But legislators eventually learned that privately owned banks are prone to periods of chronic *underissue*. Sometimes these periods are a result of exogenous economic shocks (like the COVID-19 pandemic); sometimes they result from destabilizing periods of overissue induced by financial sector profit-seeking (e.g., the subprime housing bubble).*

These monetary contractions are extremely disruptive. At their worst, they involve full-on panics, in which people abandon deposits and scramble for the small base of government-issued cash.** Deposits are especially vulnerable to panics because they are a type of money backed by a promise to pay another type of money (cash). Deposits give their holders the illusion they can trade deposits for cash whenever they want. But while small numbers of individuals can, in fact, do so, everyone cannot. As noted earlier, deposits outnumber cash roughly 18 to 1 in the US economy. The "runs" that result when everyone decides to bail on deposits can lead otherwise viable businesses to fail and throw millions of people out of work. Preventing such runs was the primary reason that most legislators supported the Federal Reserve Act in 1913, and a renewed concern about the problem in the wake of the Great Depression gave rise to a series of significant amendments to the Act in 1935. The Fed's primary mission is to keep the supply of deposits from shrinking, especially in the face of economic uncertainty or other shocks that might lead profit-motivated banks to retrench.

---

* Unlike politicians, who have an incentive to issue excess money to pay for current expenses, banks issue money only to fund loans and bonds. Accordingly, bank overissue tends to be a product of exuberance about future economic growth.

** When *governments* teeter, panics involve people exchanging government-issued coins and paper money for gold or foreign currency. Such panics plague countries with weak political institutions and warmongering neighbors. They aren't a risk in countries like the United States, where no one is concerned that the dollar might go extinct.

90   This goal also lies behind the Fed's so-called "dual mandate," which Congress added to the Federal Reserve Act in 1977. The dual mandate is a refinement of a mostly forgotten Depression-era law, the Employment Act of 1946, which in turn is a refinement on the Fed's initial stabilization remit. It charges the Fed with "maintain[ing] the long run growth of the monetary and credit aggregates commensurate with the economy's long run potential . . . to promote effectively the goals of maximum employment, stable prices, and moderate long-term interest rates."

      Today this mandate is persistently misunderstood. It is not, as the Fed has interpreted it in recent years, about achieving a steady low rate of inflation over time. It is about stimulating banks to expand the money supply at a rate sufficient to achieve full capacity utilization in the economy over the long run. It has a *single directive*—monetary expansion—and proceeds to describe the long-run macroeconomic consequences associated with that directive in terms of three variables, not two. These variables are (1) maximum employment, (2) price stability, and (3) moderate long-term interest rates. The idea is that when the economy is running at full capacity, everyone who is able to produce goods and services will have a job, prices will be stable, and the cost of borrowing money for further investment will be moderate. Bringing about these three macroeconomic conditions do not represent *direct* goals for the Fed; rather, they are the product, according to Congress, of a monetary policy that grows the money supply at a rate consistent with the economy's full potential.

      This distinction is important because there are many reasons that, in the short-to-medium term, the economy might not achieve full potential—as manifested by maximum

employment, price stability, and moderate long-term interest
rates. Often these reasons have nothing to do with monetary
expansion, the only variable Congress expected the Fed to control. For example, supply shortages of key goods and services
can cause prices to rise temporarily (meaning months or even
years). The Fed's job is not to stop these price rises, just as its
job is not to engineer long-term interest rates so that they are
"moderate."* Its job is to ensure that a lack of money created
by the banking system does not prevent the economy from
achieving these conditions over the long term.

Goal Two: Level Playing Field

Congress also established the Fed to ensure that people across
the country are able to maintain deposit accounts and borrow
new deposits into existence. Prior to the Fed's founding, the government played only a minor role in coordinating the banking
system. Most of the work was done by the banks themselves.
Smaller banks in less-populated parts of the country developed
relationships with larger banks in "money centers" like New
York and Chicago. These money center banks "cleared" payments between banks in the periphery, essentially serving as
go-betweens for small town banks and thus allowing their customers to write checks drawn on their accounts and use them to
pay for goods and services. Money center banks also lent cash to

---

* Arguments that the Fed should raise interest rates to shrink the economy to
prevent prices from rising above a certain annual rate are inconsistent with
its mandate. Rather than lead to full capacity utilization, such hikes would
stunt long-run growth by disincentivizing businesses from making the sort
of investments needed to expand their production to meet growing demand.
Such a policy, similar to what many central banks have pursued in recent
decades, can instead be expected to result in ongoing underinvestment.

92   smaller banks to help them manage short-term spikes in cus-
tomer withdrawals. Over time, money center banks grew powerful, able to influence the availability of credit in distant cities
and towns.

Policymakers recognized that without an actor like the
Fed, the diffuse network of privately owned banks would leave
some areas underserved. They were especially concerned by the
power of money center banks and their treatment of smaller
financial firms. This concern reached a fever pitch in 1912 during
the Pujo Hearings. This congressional investigation revealed
"a vast concentration of power in the hands of a few men over
the credit system of the United States." Although Congress had
created a banking system with thousands of banks to diffuse
the power of individual bankers over the economy, Democrats
in Washington were deeply worried that a few banks had figured out a way to exercise de facto control over the rest of the
banking system, undermining the American Monetary Settlement and threatening American democracy. In pressing Congress to pass the Federal Reserve Act, President Wilson asked:
"What will it profit us to be quit of one kind of monopoly [rail-
road trusts, Standard Oil, and the like] if we are to remain in the
grip of another and more effective kind?" To Wilson, the creation of the Fed was a question of freedom. The Fed, with its
network of twelve disparate Federal Reserve Banks, would make
sure banks all over the country could expand the money supply
without the permission of New York or Chicago banks.

Goal Three: Public Control and Accountability
Congress's third goal was to exert greater government control
over the banking system. For fifty years, progressive reformers

had fought to have the government reverse delegation and expand the money supply directly by issuing much more of its own currency. They objected to the fact that the most important decisions about monetary conditions were made behind closed doors in private bank boardrooms and private clearinghouses (which were associations of banks). These decisions, they pointed out, seemed to benefit private interests more than they advanced the public welfare. By 1913, the Democratic Party was no longer willing to accept a system in which "the lifeblood of commerce" was in the hands of for-profit enterprise. As one senator explained: money is "the yardstick by which all products of labor are measured. The control of this standard of value should be in the hands of the Government. . . . Any power that can control the volume of money, increasing it or decreasing it arbitrarily to serve selfish interests, has the power of life and death over American business and industry."

Correcting this is the job of the Fed's Board of Governors. The Board actively influences and limits the power of shareholder-appointed executives who issue most of the money in the country. As President Wilson explained, "The control of the system of banking . . . must be public, not private, must be vested in the Government itself, so that the banks may be the instruments, not the masters, of business and of individual enterprise and initiative." Or as one legislator explained during debate over the Federal Reserve Act,

> The great power of banking and currency, probably the mightiest tool of the people, an instrument designed to carry on the business of trade and commerce, is secured to the Government by this section. . . . I can not understand

94
    how men at all familiar with the principles of government can hesitate in deciding to place [the power] with the Government and not with the banks, because the power over the expansion and contraction of currency and credit is so great and so absolutely controls all business that as a power it must be abused if it is permitted to be exploited by selfish men or still more selfish corporations. And when abused under the form of law this power becomes tyranny and oppression.

In 1913, no other leading country in the world had a monetary system led by government officials. All had apex banks on the model of the Bank of England—privately operated quasi-monopolies that operated a general banking business. These "central banks" were like our state and national banks: their clients included nonbank financial firms, businesses, and even individuals. To the policymakers who wrote the Federal Reserve Act, the Fed was not a central bank at all. The law created *twelve* Federal Reserve Banks, limited them to interacting with banks, and, "The Federal reserve board, technically speaking, has no banking function. It is strictly a board of control, properly constituted of high Government officials, doing justice to the banks, but fairly and courageously representing the interests of the people." The government board–run Fed was the world's first monetary authority—a public organization and progressive reform.

The Fed's Tool Kit

But how is the Fed meant to achieve these goals of monetary expansion, a level playing field, and public accountability? How is it to do justice to the banks while representing the interests of the people? Congress provided the Fed a number of levers designed specifically to allow the Fed to fulfill its main aims. While the most important is the Fed's power to issue notes and deposits—to issue its own money—the Fed's printing press is designed to work in narrowly defined ways. In order to understand how the Fed is designed to deploy its power to create money, it is necessary first to understand how the Fed interfaces with the banking system on a daily basis.

The banking system facilitates trillions of dollars of transactions every day, as millions of customers from thousands of banks use their deposit accounts to make payments to each other. One of the Fed's most basic responsibilities is to help banks "clear and settle" these payments—that is, to adjust deposit account records to reflect all the transactions from customers of these different banks. The idea is to allow banks to work together as a single system, more like one big Bank of the United States than thousands of separate state and national banks.[*]

To do this—to stitch together bank balance sheets so that customers of one bank can seamlessly interact with customers of another bank—the Fed operates as a bank for banks. Banks maintain accounts at one of the twelve Federal Reserve Banks called "reserve accounts" or "master accounts." The balances in

---

[*] As one of the primary architects of the National Bank Act, Rep. Samuel Hooper, put it in 1862, the country's banks will secure "all of the benefits of the old United States Bank without many of those objectionable features which aroused opposition. . . . It will be as if the Bank of the United States had been divided into many parts, and each part endowed with the life, motion, and similitude of the whole." Congressional Globe, 37th Congress, 2nd Session, 616 (1862).

these accounts are known as "reserves" or "settlement balances." Reserve accounts are similar in many respects to the deposit accounts that ordinary people have at banks. For example, like ordinary deposit accounts, banks maintain deposit balances in their reserve accounts. Like ordinary deposit accounts, banks can withdraw cash or coin from their reserve accounts (that is, in fact, how all cash and coin enter circulation). And like ordinary deposit accounts, banks can use their reserve accounts to make transfers to other reserve accounts.

Banks make these transfers using a system called Fedwire. Fedwire is what allows ordinary people with accounts at Bank of America to pay people with accounts at Wells Fargo. Every day, thousands of customers at Bank of America write checks or send wires to people with accounts at Wells Fargo and vice versa. Wells Fargo and Bank of America figure out the net amount that Bank of America's customers owe to Wells Fargo's customers (or vice versa, depending on which bank's customers made more transfers). To help banks determine this amount, the Fed runs a nationwide check-clearing system, which adds up all the check transfers, and an electronic service known as FedACH, which processes electronic payments drawn on banks by depositors of other banks. (Banks also run an ACH service known as the Electronic Payments Network.) The Fed then allows Bank of America to settle (i.e., satisfy) its net debt to Wells Fargo by using the balance in its reserve account. To do so, Fed employees decrease the balance in Bank of America's account and increase the balance in Wells Fargo's. The Fed makes similar electronic adjustments to the account balances of all the banks in the system, with trillions of transactions between the millions of customers of American banks clearing on the Fed's books every day. In principle, it is no different than one big Excel spreadsheet.

The Fed uses this system to advance important public purposes related to its goals of stimulating monetary expansion and ensuring a level playing field among banks. First, by clearing interbank transfers on its books, the Fed allows households and businesses to treat their deposits at one bank as fungible with deposits at another, reducing the likelihood of failed payments or banks cutting each other off from the rest of the system. It is easy to overlook today, but even the possibility that some banks will exclude other banks from the payments system is destabilizing. No one wants to have deposits at a bank if other banks in the system won't accept transfers of those deposits as money. The willingness of people to treat their bank account balances as equivalent to cash depends on the willingness of other banks to interface with their bank.* By committing to facilitate the transfer of deposit balances from one bank to another without picking favorites or running for the hills when economic conditions deteriorate, the Fed helps keep things running and the money supply from contracting.

Second, the Fed leverages its position at the pivot point of the monetary system to stimulate monetary expansion. The Fed uses the fact that banks settle payments between each other

---

* Prior to the creation of the Fed, this was a serious problem. In the nineteenth century, private clearinghouses and banks sometimes changed their mind about other banks, prompting panic. For example, in 1907, private bankers induced a major panic by terminating account relationships with firms they saw as being in poor health. Depositors at the terminated firms immediately withdrew their deposits and the terminated firms rapidly shrunk their balance sheets. The panic precipitated a widespread contraction of the money supply and a sharp drop in economic output.

98   using Fed-issued reserves to influence the size and composition of bank balance sheets, most importantly, to control how many deposits banks issue. It does this by using its power to create more reserves (and their physical complement, cash) out of thin air. The Fed buys and sells financial assets by increasing (or decreasing) the amount of reserves in the banking system in order to stimulate (or impede) bank balance sheet expansion.* The Fed's goal in doing this is not, at least directly, to create more money for ordinary people to use; ordinary people cannot use reserves. Instead, the Fed's goal is to create more money for banks to use and thereby to induce banks to create more money (i.e., deposits) for ordinary people.

Adding reserves to a bank's master account enables the bank to make new loans (by adding deposits to the accounts of its customers) for two reasons. First, and most straightforwardly, Congress gave the Fed the power to require banks to hold a certain level of reserves depending on the size and composition of their balance sheets. Reserves in this way function like a quota. Banks cannot make new loans to their customers, in the process creating new deposits, if they do not have enough reserves to meet the Fed's requirements. Reserve requirements are a constraint on the banking franchise, a way for the public to put a ceiling on bank money creation.

Second, banks need reserves to settle their debts to each other. Generally speaking, the more deposits a bank issues, the more reserve balances it will need. That is because when you

---

* It also adjusts the terms on which it offers to lend reserves to banks that need them to satisfy their debts to other banks in the system. When it lends to banks, it increases the balances in their reserve accounts in exchange for the bank's promise to pay the Fed back at a later date.

wire money from your deposit account to someone who has a deposit account at another bank, your bank has to settle up with the recipient's bank using reserves.* If your bank does not have enough reserves to cover the amount of the wire, the Fed will give your bank until the end of the day to borrow reserves. One way your bank can do this is in what is known as the Federal Funds or "Fed Funds" market. The Fed Funds market is an inter-bank lending market where banks lend reserves to each other.

The interest rate in this market is what the Fed targets as part of its conventional monetary policy. Although the Fed does not raise or lower this rate directly, it can push it up and down by adjusting reserve requirements—changing the amount of reserves each bank is required to maintain, thereby changing the demand for reserves—or by adjusting the total amount of reserves in circulation, thereby changing the supply of reserves.** The Fed can also influence this interest rate by adjusting the periodic payments it makes to banks, known as "interest on reserves." These payments are a function of a bank's balance in its reserve account. When the Fed wants banks to charge more to lend out their excess reserves to other banks,

---

* For example, when Person A at Bank 1 sends a wire to Person B at Bank 2, three banks edit their records: Bank 1 reduces the account balance of Person A on its books; Bank 2 increases the account balance of Person B on its books; and the Fed adjusts its books, too, reducing the account balance of Bank 1 and increasing the account balance of Bank 2.

** To do the latter, the Fed either buys short-term Treasury securities using reserves it creates with a stroke of a keyboard or sells securities it already owns, writing down the account of the buyer. Historically, when people talked about the Fed "raising rates," typically they meant that the Fed was selling Treasury securities off its balance sheet, reducing the number of reserves in the system until the price banks pay to lend each other reserves overnight increases to the level policymakers are targeting.

100   it raises the rate it pays banks for holding onto reserves. (Similarly, when the Fed wants banks to charge less, it lowers the rate it pays banks on their reserve balances.) Think about it from the perspective of a bank: if the Fed is going to pay 1 percent every year on your reserve balance, you are going to demand more than 1 percent to lend that balance to another bank in the Fed Funds market.

Those are the three standard mechanisms (adjusting the amount of reserves in the system, adjusting reserve requirements, and adjusting interest rates on reserves) by which the Fed influences bank money creation.[*] But there are other ways that the Fed distributes its reserves to influence the money supply. For example, it also lends reserves to banks directly. In addition to the Fed Funds rate—the price banks charge each other for lending reserves around—there is a second price for reserves known as the Discount Rate. If a bank is unable to borrow reserves in the Federal Funds market, perhaps because other banks have doubts about its financial condition, that bank can turn to the Fed and borrow at the "Discount Window." The Discount Window was once the Fed's primary means of conducting monetary policy, but today the Fed uses it only as a backstop. When the Fed tries to induce banks to charge more for lending their extra reserves to other banks by using one of the mechanisms described above, it also raises the price for Discount Window loans. It sets this latter rate, however, higher than its target for the Federal Funds rate, so that in the normal

---

[*] Congress gave the Fed the power to pay interest on reserves in 2008. The Fed now relies on this mechanism as its primary means of influencing the Federal Funds rate. See Morgan Ricks, "Money as Infrastructure," *Columbia Business Law Review* (2018), pp. 757–807.

course, when a bank originates new loans and expands its balance sheet, it will borrow any extra reserves from other banks, rather than from the Fed.

That does not mean that the Discount Rate is not important. Its existence allows banks to expand their balance sheet while remaining confident that they have access to any reserves they might need. And in an economic downturn, when depositors demand cash and the interbank lending market becomes stressed or frozen, the Discount Window receives more use. In these times, the Fed acts as a "lender of last resort," preventing panic-induced declines in the money stock by providing cash to banks so that they can meet depositor withdrawals. When the Fed does this, it might seem like the Fed is "bailing out" the banks. But that misunderstands the system's design. The point of Discount Window lending is not for the government to invest in banks—to lend to banks in the way that ordinary people or banks themselves lend. Rather, it is to regulate the amount of money in the economy. The ability and willingness of banks to expand the supply of deposits by originating new loans is a function of the price banks have to pay to borrow reserves from either the Fed or other banks. The presence of the Fed's Discount Window—combined with deposit insurance, which Congress created in 1933—has practically eliminated traditional bank runs as a source of monetary contraction.

Nonbank Lending

There is another Fed lending tool, one that has received significant attention in recent years and that has the potential to operate much more like a bailout. This power, which allows the Fed to work around banks rather than through them, is codified

102   in Section 13(3) of the Federal Reserve Act. It provides that, in "unusual and exigent circumstances," the Fed's Board can authorize the Federal Reserve Banks to lend to "any participant in any program or facility with broad-based eligibility," even if the borrowers are not banks and do not have reserve accounts.

On the surface, this power seems to allow the Fed to act as a national bank rather than a monetary authority: extending credit as banks do and interacting directly with businesses, rather than regulating the supply of bank money as a monetary authority that oversees banks. But there are a variety of restrictions on this power that make it more like the Discount Window than many people assume. First, it is hard to activate. Unlike the Fed's other tools, it requires the approval of the Secretary of the Treasury and a five-vote supermajority of the Fed's Board. Second, it is designed to permit the Fed to step into the shoes of privately owned banks only when those banks are unable to do their job. Thus, before lending, 13(3) requires the Federal Reserve Banks to obtain evidence that borrowers are unable to access adequate credit accommodations from other banks (the "credit availability proviso"). Third, it requires the Fed's Board to establish policies and procedures to ensure that (1) the Federal Reserve Banks secure their loans in ways that are "sufficient to protect taxpayers from losses," (2) all borrowers are solvent, (3) loans are not designed to remove assets from the balance sheet of any single company, and (4) lending is for the purpose of providing liquidity to the financial system (the "financial system liquidity clause").

Two of these restrictions—the credit availability proviso and the financial system liquidity clause—are particularly limiting and underline the power's monetary purpose. The credit availability proviso prevents the Federal Reserve Banks from lending to households, nonprofits, municipalities, and businesses, as banks do, unless it can first obtain evidence that the banking system has ceased to function properly. The proviso was part of a compromise in 1932 between legislators who sought to empower the Reconstruction Finance Corporation, an organization created by Congress to serve as a general-purpose government lender, and President Hoover, who opposed government banking.* By adding 13(3) to the Federal Reserve Act, policymakers expected the Fed to replace lost credit in communities where banks had failed or were in such weak condition that they could not continue to lend to their existing customers. In other words, Congress extended the Fed's administrative role in the banking system to include the task of ensuring that customers of damaged banks can still access credit.

Congress added the other major restriction on 13(3), the financial system liquidity clause, in 2010. This clause scales back the circumstances in which Federal Reserve Banks can bypass the banking system by limiting the Fed to lending for the purpose of providing liquidity to the financial system. This requirement rules out most (if not all) lending to households and businesses, even where the Fed is able to obtain evidence that borrowers are unable to access adequate credit

---

* According to Hoover, "[T]he fatal difficulty is . . . [the] provision that loans should also be made to individuals, private corporations, partnerships, States, and municipalities on any conceivable security and for every purpose. Such an undertaking by the United States Government makes the Reconstruction Corporation the most gigantic banking and pawnbroking business in all history." Herbert Hoover, Statement on Emergency Relief and Construction Legislation, July 6, 1932.

104   accommodations from banks. In essence, Section 13(3) today permits the Fed to lend to nonbank financial firms when their access to funding from the banking system dries up, just as it uses the Discount Window to lend to banks that are unable to borrow from other banks in the Federal Funds markets. It is a nod by Congress to the reality of shadow banking and the important role its money claims play in the economy.

To summarize, the Fed is built to act through banks. This explains why, in 2008, the chairman of the House Finance Committee wondered where the Fed would obtain the $80 billion it proposed to lend to AIG. At that point in time, few people realized that the Fed's printing press could be used to assist firms without bank charters. The next chapter turns to how the rise of shadow banking led understandings to shift, putting increasing pressure on the statutory design and prompting the Fed to explicitly support enterprises outside of the banking system and expand its balance sheet.

The Collapse of Banking Law

If the Federal Reserve is set up to function as a limited purpose monetary authority that administers the size of bank balance sheets, how did it come to play a leading role in the government's response to the COVID-19 pandemic? The Fed's recent actions have been, in many respects, driven by the changing structure of monetary and financial activity. They are an attempt to hold together a fraying system and reverse the economic damage wrought by that system since 2008. The principal problem giving rise to the Fed Unbound is shadow banking. Over the past half century, wealthy individuals, businesses, and institutional investors have increasingly turned to alternative forms of money, issued neither by chartered banks nor by the government. These moneys are similar to deposits yet structured to evade the legal restrictions that forbid companies without bank charters from issuing deposits. The workarounds include instruments ordinary people rarely encounter, such as repurchase agreements, eurodollars, and financial and asset-backed commercial paper, as well as more familiar instruments like money market mutual funds. Perhaps the primary appeal of these alternative forms of money is that (in good times) they offer higher interest to their holders than deposits issued by banks. But in bad times people often lose confidence in them—because they are not backed by the government in the ways deposits are—leading to runs on the shadow banks that issue them. The result is the same as when people lose confidence in chartered banks and rush to redeem their deposits: monetary contraction and recession.

The Fed's 2008 rescue of the shadow bank Bear Stearns, which began a period of escalating assistance for such firms and culminated in 2020's $3 trillion backstop, was about preventing precisely the sort of economic collapse that Congress created the Fed to prevent. Later that same year, when the Fed decided not to aid a different shadow bank, Lehman Brothers, it worsened a contraction that eventually cost the economy millions of jobs and as much as $22 trillion in lost economic output, roughly a year's worth of GDP. To achieve its congressionally mandated goal—monetary expansion sufficient to foster full capacity utilization across the economy over the long term—the Fed may find it needs to preserve widely used alternative forms of money when people lose confidence in their issuers.

One of the side effects of this dynamic is that these forms of money are able to persist and expand. Indeed, the expectation that the Fed will be there in a crunch is generally required for privately issued money to attract holders in the first place. And, as we will see, the Fed played a pivotal role in allowing deposit alternatives to emerge at scale, as it nurtured many shadow banks during the second half of the twentieth century and helped them to erode the safeguards Congress built into the American Monetary Settlement during the New Deal. In

this way, the Fed's balance sheet today is a manifestation of radical changes that took place decades ago and the acute impact of
those changes in 2008. This chapter reviews this transformation and explains how it gave rise to our current predicament.

Shadow Banking: Dealer Repo

The first shadow banks to emerge were the firms that Congress
most sought to separate from the monetary system during the
Great Depression: broker dealers, also known as "investment
banks." At the heart of the New Deal banking system is a provision that prohibits broker dealers, along with any company or
individual that is not regulated as a bank, from issuing deposit
liabilities to the public. Congress adopted this stricture, which
is still in effect, in 1933. Its goal was to prevent a repeat of the
worst monetary contraction in American history by ensuring
that banking activities were never again able to escape the government's regulatory perimeter. Legislators were particularly
concerned with the role of broker dealers, which conduct a range
of activities that government-chartered banks have long been
legally forbidden from undertaking: they buy and sell securities
issued by businesses and governments; issue or "underwrite"
new securities on behalf of businesses and governments; and
advise businesses and governments on how best to raise capital.

During the 1920s, many banks affiliated with broker dealers
in order to circumvent laws preventing banks from engaging in
this sort of financial commerce. This conglomeration concentrated money and credit resources, fueled financial speculation,
and helped bring down one-third of the banking system. Upon
taking office in 1933, Franklin D. Roosevelt pressed Congress
to separate banks from these sorts of businesses once again.

108   The result—the Glass-Steagall Act—forced banks and broker dealers to divorce.

Later that same year, Congress also set up a new regulatory regime for broker dealers, firms that the federal government had not previously overseen. The capstone of this regime is the Securities and Exchange Commission, or SEC, an independent commission that Congress created in a separate piece of legislation. The SEC-led legal framework for broker dealers, which focuses on investor protection and efficient capital markets, is quite different from the regulatory regime that applies to banks. While it attempts to improve disclosure practices by firms seeking to raise money by selling securities, it neither closely monitors the financial risks broker dealers take on their balance sheets, nor provides broker dealers with access to government backstopping. It presupposes that broker dealers finance their activities not by issuing money claims, but by borrowing money from investors for extended periods of time or by issuing stock to shareholders who do not demand fixed periodic interest payments. As far as the monetary system is concerned, the banking laws presume that broker dealers are like everyone else in the economy.

In the 1950s, however, a group of Wall Street dealers began to reenter the banking business. Their technique was to use a type of financial transaction that functions like a deposit but is not structured like one. These "nondeposit deposits," known as repurchase agreements, or repos, are formally a pair of transactions—a purchase and a sale of a financial asset. A party known as a "cash provider" buys a debt security from a party known as a "cash borrower." The cash provider (the depositor) pays for the security using a commercial bank deposit. The cash borrower (the shadow bank) takes the provider's cash and give them a new liability, which they can also treat as equivalent to cash.

But cash providers and cash borrowers do not execute a genuine sale. The cash provider does not pay a market price for the security; it pays less than the security is worth to protect itself in case the security loses value. Nor does the cash provider receive an economic interest in the security it buys; under the agreement, any change in value of the security ultimately accrues to the cash borrower (the party that putatively sold the security). Moreover, both parties agree that at some point in the future, usually the next day, the cash provider will sell the debt security back for a prearranged price and that any income earned by the debt security in the interim will go to the cash borrower. In other words, a repo involves a sale in name only, conducted by the parties to get around the legal prohibition on nonbanks maintaining deposit accounts. Repos also offer the cash provider an attractive form of specific collateral, the security. The cash provider has a legal right to it, which, in theory, it can exercise if it ever asks the cash borrower for its cash back and the cash borrower defaults. You can think of the security as a type of deposit insurance, an alternative to the system the government runs to ensure that people don't have to worry about whether banks will be able to pay cash to their depositors.

Repos function as cash equivalents because, in much the same way that depositors at government-chartered banks rarely draw down their account balances and ask their bank for cash, repo holders at unchartered shadow banks rarely "sell" back their security. Instead, they "roll over" the arrangement and let the shadow bank keep the money. In this way, shadow banks expand the money supply just like banks. Before the repo, the

110   cash provider had a deposit at a commercial bank. After the repo, the shadow bank has a deposit at a commercial bank and the cash provider has a repo, which it treats as a deposit at a commercial bank (and can account for as a deposit on its balance sheet). By entering into repos with cash providers (usually institutional investors with large deposit balances at banks), dealers seek the benefit of financing themselves by sating some of the economy's money demand—i.e., by eating into the profitable banking franchise—without having to comply with the costly restrictions that the government imposes on banks.

It is doubtful that the dealers would have succeeded in developing this business on their own. After all, in a repo, when a cash provider decides not to roll over, they are in the same position as a bank depositor seeking to withdraw cash. And the cash borrower is in a similar position to a bank that needs a Federal Reserve Bank deposit to clear a payment at one of the Federal Reserve Banks. But whereas banks have the Discount Window to obtain any reserves they need, dealers do not. They have banks, and banks are not always willing to lend. In a period of economic contraction, a repo is a pale imitation of a bank deposit: If you are a cash provider, why use a repo issued by a firm that lacks access to cash?

Dealer repo was facilitated by the government—indeed, by the Fed itself. Congress had no intention of repealing the Glass-Steagall Act. As mentioned, its provisions prohibiting nonbanks from engaging in the business of receiving deposits are still in effect today. But in the 1950s, William McChesney Martin Jr.—the chairman of the Federal Reserve Board, a former partner of a broker dealer, and a former president of the New York Stock Exchange—thought that broker dealers ought to play a

more central role in the monetary and financial system. Under
Martin's leadership, the Fed offered select broker dealers access
to overnight loans in the form of repos. In other words, it opened
an ersatz Discount Window for broker dealers. With such an
arrangement in place, cash providers seeking to unwind their
repos could rest easy knowing that the broker dealers on the other
side had access to cash from the Fed, just like banks. These "primary dealers" became de facto franchisees of the central bank.

The Federal Reserve was not set up to facilitate dealer repo,
and members of Congress raked Martin over the coals in 1957.
The Fed "is right now doing something which I do not consider to
be legal at all," said the chairman of the House Banking and Currency Committee, Wright Patman. "They are permitting dealers
in Government securities to borrow money directly from the
New York Federal Reserve Bank." According to Patman, the "Federal Reserve banks were set up to accommodate member banks,"
not broker dealers. Patman was incensed to "find a half dozen
dealers—not over fifteen—in the city of New York who get their
money directly from the Federal Reserve to speculate in Government securities." Not only was this unfair and dangerous, but
"[t]here is nothing in the Federal Reserve Act . . . that permits
them to borrow money from the Federal Reserve for that purpose."

Martin responded to Patman's attack by asking Congress
to amend the law. But Congress never did. And the Fed continued to support dealer repo. Repo allowed dealers to operate
at lower cost, which helped them to expand the market for corporate securities and reduce the cost to investors of buying and
selling securities. (Securities markets grew during this period
so that large corporations could raise large amounts of money
directly from savers, which proved easier for these corporations

112   than borrowing money from banks, given the diffuse design of the banking system.) Repo also offered the Fed a way to support the US Treasury market. By lending to primary dealers, the Fed assisted the dealers in smoothing fluctuations in the demand for government debt, making it cheaper and easier for dealers to step in and buy Treasury bonds when end investors failed to absorb all of the bonds the government sought to sell. (This in turn helped the Fed to avoid pressure from the Treasury Department to support the Treasury market directly, as it had during the Second World War.) It was a stalemate.

Dealer shadow banking, however, remained modest in scope for many years, with Fed support limited to those primary dealers that helped the Treasury Department borrow in the capital markets. The explosion of repo banking, and the development of a large-scale "repo market" that operates as an analog to the Federal Funds market, did not materialize until the 1990s.

One of the major catalysts came in 1991, when Congress loosened restrictions on the Fed's emergency lending powers so that the Fed could more easily backstop broker dealers in the case of a large-scale panic. This amendment to Section 13(3) of the Federal Reserve Act made it easier for the broker dealers to fund themselves using repos, because it made cash providers more confident that repos would function like bank deposits during periods of economic stringency. In other words, by working to protect the overall system from the dangers of dealers, the 1991 amendment made dealers more like banks.

Shadow Banking: Eurodollars

Congressional acquiescence to the rise of repo had other consequences. In 1962, less than five years after Martin's exchange with Patman, the Martin-led Fed threw its support behind another alternative form of money known as a eurodollar. A eurodollar is a dollar-denominated deposit issued overseas by a company outside the jurisdiction of US law and without a US banking charter. (Eurodollars have nothing to do with euros, the currency.*) Like a repurchase agreement or bank deposit in the US, a eurodollar is an agreement in which one party, the issuer, is on the hook to pay the other party dollars on demand or within a short period of time. The simplest type of eurodollar is a bank account balance denominated in dollars, just like a normal deposit, but maintained by a bank outside of the United States. Today, financial institutions around the world, including nonbanks like insurance companies, issue eurodollars in various forms, including as repurchase agreements.

Eurodollars are an arbitrage, a way for companies to issue dollar money instruments without complying with US banking laws.** Eurodollar issuers are not chartered by the US government, nor are they insured by the Federal Deposit Insurance Corporation. Often, the firms that issue eurodollars do not have access to the Discount Window. When the customers of these firms demand dollars, these firms typically draw down bank

---

* The name derives from one of the banks that pioneered the practice of maintaining dollar-denominated deposit balances without a US banking charter: the Paris-based, Soviet-owned Banque Commerciale pour L'Europe du Nord known as "Eurobank." Anthony Sampson, *The Money Lenders: Bankers and a World in Turmoil* (1982), p. 109.

** The first overseas dollar deposits were used by the Chinese and Soviet governments to evade US sanctions and legal processes. The market grew as a way to skirt US restrictions on bank balance sheets, interest rate controls, deposit insurance requirements, and US taxes. See Paul Einzig, *The Euro-Dollar System* (1970).

accounts that they maintain with banks in the US (institutions that *do* have access to the Discount Window). When these firms deplete their correspondent accounts (their own US commercial bank deposits), they borrow from other financial institutions with positive balances in what is known as the eurodollar market.

Eurodollar markets, and the total number of eurodollars, were tiny at first, likely for the same reason that dealer repo had been: What happens if demand for dollars spikes and eurodollar issuers draw down their dollar reserves at US banks? If US banks are not willing to lend, these foreign firms must turn to their own governments and central banks. But unlike the Federal Reserve, foreign monetary authorities cannot expand the supply of physical dollars. In lending dollars, foreign monetary authorities are limited by the balances they hold in their own accounts at the Fed. (Foreign central banks have accounts at the Fed just like domestic banks.)

During the 1960s and 1970s, the Fed decided to provide support for eurodollar issuers. Seeking to fuel an unregulated overseas financial market, in the hope that fewer restrictions on cross-border finance would ultimately provide an advantage to US banks, the Fed set up swap lines with other central banks: ersatz Discount Windows for foreign monetary authorities so that they could backstop the firms in their jurisdictions issuing dollar deposits. To recall the discussion in chapter 1, swap lines are lending programs: The Fed lends dollars to a foreign central bank by increasing that bank's account balance at the Fed (creating new money out of thin air). The foreign central bank, in exchange for raising its balance at the Fed, credits on its books an account in the name of the Fed. The banks swap currencies.

The eurodollar market, from the start, was more fragile than dealer repo: the Fed had less of an idea who was creating these dollar moneys, and different countries had different rules governing their creation. Eurodollar depositors had little sense of the extent of the Fed's commitment to overseas issuers. Predictably, after steadily expanding for a decade, eurodollar markets went haywire in the face of economic trouble. The problem was related to rising oil prices in 1973–74. But the eurodollar market would probably not have been able to survive any shock large enough to cause a sustained fall in asset prices; as asset prices fall, asset owners often need or desire actual deposits. Alternative forms of money like eurodollars will no longer do.

The Fed was not designed to backstop foreign central banks or foreign banks issuing dollar deposits because, as mentioned, its architects assumed that only domestic banks would engage in this sort of activity. But after the 1974 eurodollar turmoil helped bring down a domestic bank participating in the market,* the Fed issued a communiqué along with central banks in nine other countries, promising to funnel enough dollars to foreign central banks so that they could backstop banks in their jurisdiction issuing dollar-denominated deposits. The release was spare, but it was interpreted by market participants to mean that dollar deposits created overseas would enjoy a status similar in some respects to domestic deposits (even though this market was explicitly designed to circumvent US banking laws).

* The run on Franklin National Bank, a large US bank active in the overseas eurodollar market that also funded itself by entering into repos, was the first since the New Deal. Franklin had a bank charter, and so had access to the Fed's Discount Window. Nevertheless, it foundered when cash providers ran on its eurodollars and repos, a sequence of events very similar to what would befall Lehman Brothers in 2008.

116   The panic subsided. And in the years that followed, the euro-
         dollar market grew enormously, sapping demand for US bank
         deposits and further undermining the bank franchise.

Shadow Banking: Money Market Funds

A third major alternative form of money emerged in the 1970s,
when the Securities and Exchange Commission authorized a
new variety of investment vehicle, the money market mutual
fund. Money market mutual funds issue shares. Technically,
money fund shareholders own an equity stake in an investment fund. But SEC rules permit the shares to maintain a $1 net
asset value even if the prices of the underlying assets fluctuate
slightly—meaning that in good times each share tends to be
worth one dollar. As a result, holders treat these shares the same
as cash on their balance sheets, and they expect that they will be
able to redeem them for US bank deposits at any time.

The appeal of money fund shares to customers is that they
earn higher interest rates than government-regulated bank
deposits (just like repos and eurodollars). When money funds
started, their primary customers were retail investors who were
earning substantially less interest on their bank account balances due to overly restrictive bank regulatory policies in the
1970s that limited the rate of interest banks were allowed to pay.
Later, when these policies were changed, money funds began to
cater to institutional investors who were attracted to these products even when the difference in interest rates was narrower.

Unsurprisingly, as with dealer repo and eurodollars, money
market funds have proved to be unstable during periods of economic stringency. To persuade people to hold money fund
shares instead of deposits (or dealer repo or eurodollars), money

market funds tend to maintain portfolios of short-term debt issued by highly regarded companies and financial institutions. But since money fund shares are backed only by the assets in the fund, even the prospect of a default on one of these assets can shatter the expectation that they will be redeemable for deposits at par.

A Run on the Shadow Banks

By 2008, shadow banks were issuing more money than banks. American commerce was fueled by roughly $15 trillion worth of repos, eurodollars, commercial paper, and money market funds, $7 trillion in commercial bank deposits, and $1 trillion in physical cash and coin. Although alternative forms of money created by shadow banks were inherently unstable, issued by firms without the financial strength and government supervision of banks, they sated a huge portion of the money demand, and the economy depended on them to function.

The problem has to do with the way the money supply affects productive activity. An economy of a certain size—with a certain volume of transactions and number of participants—requires a certain amount of money to operate. Some money is used as a medium of exchange, as a way to pay for things. Households and businesses, for example, use money to settle bills as they come due. And if they don't have enough money coming in—in the form of salary or interest income or revenues—then they will need to borrow money from a bank or else declare bankruptcy. Other money is used as a store of value: households and businesses will hold money as a "transaction reserve," so that they don't have to worry about shortfalls in their salary, interest income, or revenues.

118   If the supply of money drops, and the demand for money stays the same, all else equal, prices fall. In response, households will compete to get their hands on whatever money is available in order to pay their bills and maintain their transaction reserves. This dynamic makes it harder for people to pay for things: they have less money, so they can pay less. It also raises the cost of borrowing money.

When shadow banks go bankrupt, the alternative forms of money they issue disappear from the system. Anyone holding their nondeposit deposits is left, at best, with the collateral (say from the repo transaction), and, at worst, in a legal proceeding trying to get paid out. Even if their wealth does not decrease, they no longer have as much *money* as they previously did— that is, they have fewer instruments they can use to make payments or hold as transaction reserves. They are thus likely to demand money from somewhere else and look to sell something in exchange for a bank deposit or other form of money.

If banks don't step in and expand their balance sheets, issuing new deposits to make up for the alternative forms of money that were lost, the price level will fall. Sometimes banks *do* step in. They lend to shadow banks by offering deposits (in much the same way that the Federal Reserve Banks lend reserves at the Discount Window). But banks are motivated by profit, not public welfare, and sometimes the demand for deposits will exceed the ability or willingness of banks to supply them. In such a situation, borrowing costs will increase. In a panic, cash providers in repos tend to run on cash borrowers, eager to replace their repos with more reliable forms of money, such as commercial bank deposits backed by the Fed through the Discount Window. In this situation, cash borrowers face extinction, and the demand for more money overwhelms the ability and willingness of commercial banks to provide additional deposits, shrinking the money supply. A collapse in the money supply then leads prices to fall, interest rates to rise, businesses to fail, and people to lose their jobs.

This is what happened in 2008. Lehman Brothers, one of the largest shadow banks, fell to a classic bank run. Lehman had over sixty repo "depositors" in August 2008 with balances exceeding $150 billion in total. Two weeks later, Lehman had fewer than ten depositors remaining with balances less than $50 billion in total. Lehman's depositors panicked, leaving Lehman for dead and looking to hold forms of money issued by other firms.

The Fed struggled to adapt, caught off-guard by the problem presented by shadow banks like Lehman. Many policymakers prior to 2008 believed that repo and eurodollar markets were self-regulating and that there was nothing particularly dangerous about these alternative forms of money. But, once the panic started, the Fed realized that it had to act or else risk a second Great Depression. In a series of unprecedented interventions, reviewed in the introduction, the Fed backstopped many shadow banks (and banks that had become highly intertwined with the shadow banking system). The Fed supported AIG, Bear Stearns, Citigroup, and Bank of America. It also lent hundreds of billions of dollars to broker dealers and overseas dollar issuers (via foreign central banks). When push came to shove, shadow banks discovered they could have their cake and eat it too: they could create alternative forms of money without a bank franchise (and without the accompanying government supervision), but still have the government recognize and protect their money as if they did.

120   Backstopping Shadow Banks

When the panic subsided, many treated the episode as a hundred-year flood. Others thought the Dodd-Frank Wall Street Reform and Consumer Protection Act of 2010 would fix the problem. A decade later, we know that both views were too optimistic. After 2008, little was done to legally restrict shadow banking. Moreover, markets had learned that the Fed is highly incentivized to assist shadow banks during periods of stringency. As a result, much of what happened in 2008 repeated itself in 2020. As we saw in chapter 1, panic broke out and the Fed used an alphabet soup of ad hoc facilities to stop it. Each of the Fed's facilities served as an ersatz Discount Window supporting a different type of shadow bank. The Fed's Repurchase Operations and Primary Dealer Credit Facility accommodated the primary dealers and their repo money.[*] The Commercial Paper Funding Facility and Money Market Mutual Fund Liquidity Facility stopped runs on money funds and commercial paper issuers. And fourteen swap lines and the Foreign and International Monetary Authorities Repo Facility—the same backstops that the Fed pioneered in 1962 and pledged to use in 1974—calmed runs overseas.

---

[*] When the pandemic started, the Fed was already accommodating the primary dealers through ad hoc repurchase operations, which it had started on September 17, 2019. For regulatory, business, and operational reasons, the cost of borrowing commercial bank deposits overnight in the repo market had spiked eight points above the Federal Funds rate. As mentioned in the introduction, the Fed stepped in to prevent a full-fledged panic, ultimately lending hundreds of billions of dollars. This episode is an important example of how the Fed's backstopping role has grown beyond a crisis-times policy. While the Fed has no explicit remit to support repo market rates, the reality is that a large fraction of economic activity depends on these cash substitutes and the Fed was led to act even during a period of economic calm.

When these actions proved insufficient to hold the system together, the Fed went even further. It made over $1.5 trillion in market-functioning purchases, buying up the sorts of assets that shadow banks were selling or had sitting on their balance sheets. It signaled that financial firms that could not, or did not want to, borrow from or through the Fed could sell their most liquid assets (directly or indirectly) to the Fed. Prices stabilized.

In effect, the Fed's efforts to avert the pandemic panic extended its classic "lender of last resort" function to the shadow banking system. While the Fed lacks the tools to control the expansion and contraction of shadow bank balance sheets during normal times, it is relatively well equipped to backstop them in a crisis. With its experience setting up multiple ersatz Discount Windows in 2008, the Fed was able to react quickly. Its facilities involved minimal risk of loss to the Fed and were highly scalable: a relatively small amount of lending can prop up giant markets. Once the Fed announces that it will backstop a promise to pay dollars, those promises—whether structured as repurchase agreements or eurodollars—are as good as dollars. Often, an announcement is all it takes to stop a run.[*]

---

[*] Policymakers have been aware of this dynamic since 1847 when the British government agreed to advance a bill in Parliament that would authorize the Bank of England to expand its balance sheet. That news ended a crippling panic within hours. It was not even necessary to pass the bill. As Curzio Giannini explains, "The experience [with the bank bill in 1847] provided irrefutable proof that [bank] panics could be overcome even without a sharp increase in [the base] money supply, provided prompt and firm action were taken to restore market confidence." See Curzio Giannini, *The Age of Central Banks* (2011), p. 88.

Today, market participants presume that the Fed is no less committed to shadow banks than it is to ordinary government-chartered banks, despite the fact that shadow banks exist beyond the regulatory regime meant to steer bank activities toward public purposes. During the 2008 panic, the Fed improvised, and market participants did not know what to expect; the second time around, in 2020, the dance was already choreographed. Backstopping shadow banks during periods of economic uncertainty is now part of standard Fed operating procedure.

The Fed's shadow bank backstops are both a blessing and a curse. In the short run, they have saved the economy from collapse. In the long run, they have deleterious consequences. One of those consequences is a Fed Unbound. As the Fed has stretched its buying and lending powers to provide unprecedented support to financial firms, pressure has risen for the Fed to turn these tools to support struggling homeowners, businesses, municipalities, and nonprofits—tasks for which it is not designed, and which it is unlikely to discharge effectively. Adding to this pressure is the damage to the economy caused by shadow banks in 2008, which the Fed has been unable to reverse through conventional means. In 2020, the Fed's new responsibilities took two forms: a battery of lending facilities that targeted businesses, nonprofits, and municipalities, as well as a supercharged asset purchase program, QE Infinity. Both initiatives helped blunt the adverse effects of the pandemic, but the benefits were not distributed equally. Understanding why, and the other ways that the post-2008 period is straining the Fed, is the topic of the next chapter.

What to Make of a Fed Unbound

Policymakers and commentators have responded to the Fed Unbound in a variety of ways. Some see nothing wrong: the Fed, in their view, is an economic regulator doing its part to respond to a series of pressing challenges. Others regard some of the Fed's new activities, like backstopping shadow banking and lubricating financial markets, as sensible extensions of its core mission, but see more recent initiatives, like lending to state and local governments, as potentially dangerous. The Fed is a "Supreme Court of Finance," properly intertwined with financial markets, but not designed to interact directly with ordinary households and businesses. This corporatist approach imagines the Fed as a central bank on the model of Bagehot's Bank of England—a state-backed support system for the financial sector.

More recently, both in the academy and in Congress, a new attitude toward central banking has emerged. It bemoans the Fed's need to backstop privately issued alternative forms of money, but embraces the idea that Fed officials might use their

124   printing press to solve a range of nonmonetary economic problems. Proponents of this view, mostly coming from the political left, are uninterested in what the legislature was trying to achieve when it wrote and revised the Federal Reserve Act; like the corporatist mainstream, they read the law loosely (or would like to amend it). Instead, this group sees a relatively unrestrained central bank as a salutary evolution that can bypass political logjams and direct social resources toward policy priorities they favor.

This attitude is in part the product of the Fed's track record over past fourteen years. Using its balance sheet, the Fed *has* tackled many serious policy problems. It has helped homeowners make their mortgage payments, aided businesses and municipalities trying to meet payroll, and twice prevented a second Great Depression. But an unbound Fed has costs as well, costs that have often been overlooked or underappreciated. This chapter aims to bring these costs into focus, so that we can properly evaluate whether it would be wise to further expand the scope of this increasingly important institution.

Unsettling the American Monetary Settlement

First and foremost, the Fed's efforts since 2008 to support the shadow banking system have undermined what remains of the New Deal banking system. Large-scale, Fed-backed alternative forms of money flout the safeguards legislators put in place to ensure that monetary outsourcing does not jeopardize democratic government or threaten the Constitution's egalitarian commitments.

For example, shadow banking evades the long-standing goal of separating monetary activities from ordinary commerce.

The reason is simple: shadow banks are not subject to the same
restrictions as banks. As a result, they often engage in activities off limits to banks. By mixing monetary expansion (with a
de facto government backstop) and ordinary commerce, shadow
banks drive traditional commercial firms out of certain sectors. Prior to 2008, the canonical example of this phenomenon
was General Electric, which gained a competitive edge in many
industrial markets by operating a large financial subsidiary.
Today, hedge funds like Citadel routinely finance themselves in
the repo market while engaging in a range of financial and nonfinancial businesses, including IT and insurance.

The Fed Unbound also undermines principles of diffusion.
Congress designed the banking laws to allow anyone to apply for
a charter to expand the money supply. Legislators did not want
the bank franchise to be a special privilege reserved for politically connected elites. But today's small number of primary
dealers are de facto monetary franchisees with access to the Fed
on bespoke terms. Moreover, the facilities the Fed uses to support alternative forms of money are ad hoc. Congress requires
that the Fed treat all member banks equally at the Discount
Window, but no law determines who will benefit from the Fed's
facilities and who will not.*

Fears of favoritism are heightened by the fact that the
shadow banking sector concentrates financial power. The rise of
alternative forms of money, backed by the Fed, has undercut the
profitability of smaller community banks and made it harder for

---

* In 2008, for example, the Fed lent to support Bear Stearns and AIG but not
Lehman Brothers. This dynamic was also in evidence in 2020, when, at a
sectoral level, the Fed lent in ways that favored large corporations over state
and local governments.

them to expand. In a landscape of increasingly large banks and shadow banks, further consolidation follows. Today, the size of the largest banks as a percentage of total banking assets is at its highest since Andrew Jackson vetoed the renewal of the Bank of the United States. Even large regional banks have fallen away. Places like Houston and Los Angeles lack a local champion, leaving their businesses subject instead to credit decisions made in cities like San Francisco and New York. This consolidation has redistributed credit toward Wall Street and made it harder for local entrepreneurs to borrow. It has likely also alienated people from the financial system, which seems ever more remote.

Just as worryingly, shadow banking bypasses supervision and reduces public accountability in the monetary system. Since before the Civil War, bank supervision has been a core feature of American banking law. Special government officials endowed with expansive remedial powers have regulated companies that expand the money supply to ensure that they advance the public welfare. But most shadow banks are not supervised. The Fed cannot oversee their balance sheets or activities.* Nor are

---

* There is an important exception: the Fed is able to supervise the broker dealer subsidiaries of bank holding companies and firms designated by the Financial Stability Oversight Council (FSOC) as systemically important. Before 2008, there were a series of major "independent" broker dealers (of which Bear Stearns and Lehman Brothers were two); many of those firms were forced to sell themselves to bank holding companies, which created a statutory basis for Fed oversight. Others, notably Goldman Sachs and Morgan Stanley, voluntarily converted to bank holding company status to end speculation about whether they might end up like Lehman Brothers—unable to access Fed cash facilities. This arrangement is fragile: there is no legal barrier to independent broker dealers reemerging; there is only FSOC designation, which is practically difficult to effect.

shadow banks covered by laws like the Community Reinvest-   127
ment Act, which require that banks fairly distribute the benefits
from monetary expansion. Indeed, the government even lacks
adequate awareness of what many shadow banks are doing.
While banks are subject to a rigorous reporting regime, shadow
banks are not. The Fed does not know, for example, exactly how
much repo is taking place or how many eurodollars are circulating. Nor do Fed officials know what sorts of firms are participating in these markets or in what sorts of assets they are
investing. Many shadow banks are truly in the shadows.

The Fed's QE and real economy lending initiatives also
depart from the American Monetary Settlement by diminishing
the role of the banking system. These programs do not expand
or contract the supply of bank money in the system; their effects
on monetary aggregates are indirect and analogous to the effects
that fiscal policy has on bank balance sheet expansion. Instead,
they transform the Fed from a monetary authority that administers a system of privately owned, publicly chartered banks
into a government bank that operates directly in the economy.
Asset purchase programs (and, in certain circumstances, real
economy lending facilities) empower a small group of technocrats to allocate credit between various productive purposes. In
certain instances, this may seem a good thing. But the concentration of powers it entails is precisely what generations of policymakers rejected. Legislative bodies, which are designed to be
more responsive to the public, are better suited to make decisions about high-level credit policy, and these policies could
be carried out by thousands of different bankers spread across
the country or by specially chartered government investment
authorities.

128   **Legality**

Given the importance of the American Monetary Settlement in the creation of the Fed, it is unsurprising that the Fed Unbound also stretches the Fed's statutory bindings. The Fed's most problematic moves are long-standing and involve bypassing banks to lend directly to other financial firms. Perhaps the Fed's own General Counsel put it best when, in 1923, he wrote: "It was never contemplated by Congress that the Federal reserve banks should make direct loans to non-member banks nor to stock, bond, and acceptance brokers, or other individuals, partnerships, or corporations which ordinarily would seek such accommodations from member banks." When Congress adjusted the law in 1932 to permit the Fed to bypass banks in unusual and exigent circumstances, it attached strict limits.

Yet, beginning in the Martin era, the Fed looked past these limits and structured backstops for broker dealers and overseas central banks as purchases and sales (repos and swaps) rather than loans, giving rise to the repo market and the eurodollar market. Since then, as financial firms have teetered and political pressures mounted, the Fed has leaned more and more heavily on this strained interpretation of the law. Even though the Fed's 2020 repo operations and swap lines are plainly lending programs, the Fed continues to justify them by reference to its purchasing authorities, which are set forth in Section 14 of the Federal Reserve Act. Section 14 authorizes the Fed to buy and sell government debt and foreign currency, but it requires that the Fed do so in "the open market." An open market purchase or sale is a purchase or sale at a market price. This openness

requirement ensures nonprejudicial access to the Fed's business and that the Fed's purchases take place at arm's length.*

More importantly, even if there were no "open market"
requirement and the Fed had the authority under Section 14 to
conduct off-market purchases and sales, the function of the Fed's
trades is to lend money to the Fed's counterparties and therefore
structural legal principles suggest that the procedural requirements governing Fed lending should apply. Those requirements
are set out in Section 13 and a series of rules written by the Board
known as Regulation A. And yet the Fed does not abide by these
rules for its repo operations or swap lines. Last year, when it lent
$450 billion to broker dealers and $450 billion to foreign central banks, sums that dwarf the rest of its pandemic lending, the
Fed did not secure prior approval from the Treasury Secretary or
charge a penalty rate, as required by those provisions.

Meanwhile, the Fed's credit programs for nonfinancial
firms, though they fulfilled these requirements, were in ten-
sion with other provisions of the Federal Reserve Act. Under
changes made in 2010, Congress required the Board to ensure
that the Fed's emergency lending is for the purpose of providing
liquidity to the financial system. Under long-standing law, the

---

* Neither of the transactions in a repo or a swap execute at a market price. The
initial purchase price is below market. The difference is known as the haircut
and protects the Fed from fluctuations in the value of the collateral during
the course of the loan. And the sale price is above the purchase price—the
difference is the interest rate, the Fed's profit from extending the loan. In
fact, in the case of a repo, arguably neither leg is even a "sale" or a "purchase"
within the meaning of Section 14, as full ownership rights do not transfer
(e.g., the "seller" is entitled to keep any interest payments on the underlying
security) and the repurchase is the settlement of a forward transaction.

130   Fed is also required to obtain evidence that credit is not available from other banks and that borrowers are not insolvent,
requirements that do not mesh with Fed bond buying on the
open market or Fed purchases of bond mutual funds.

For these reasons, it is unlikely that the Fed would have set
up these programs without action from Congress. Congress
explicitly sought them and, in passing the CARES Act, gave the
Fed legal authority to establish them. Unfortunately, Congress
did so by bending the law rather than amending it. The CARES
Act left the inconsistent Federal Reserve Act provisions intact,
further obscuring the extent of the Fed's authority. We now find
ourselves in a situation in which it is no longer clear which Federal Reserve Act requirements still apply to Fed programs. Nor
do we know whether and to what extent the Fed is permitted to
restart similar lending in the future, after the CARES Act appropriations expire. What sort of facilities can the Fed characterize
as being "for the purpose of providing liquidity to the financial
system"? In the absence of further legislative pronouncements,
disagreement is likely to result.

Effectiveness

Setting aside legal questions, there is also a practical problem
with the government relying on the Fed to backstop shadow
banks, compensate for inadequate fiscal policy, and extend credit
to the real economy. It isn't well designed to perform these functions. Compared to most administrative agencies, its officials are
highly insulated from political oversight, and its activities are not
subject to rigorous procedural requirements or public scrutiny.

As we saw in chapter 2, the Fed is built to administer the
banking system in a way that ensures there is enough money in

the economy to support maximum employment, price stability,
and moderate long-term interest rates. Legislators thought
that this mission entailed an unusual degree of independence
from both the courts and the president. Accordingly, many of
the Fed's activities are not subject to the same sort of judicial
review as the activities of other government agencies, nor is
its policymaking process structured with as much public participation and engagement. The Fed's mission also requires a
close relationship to the banking sector and a set of tools that
are financial in nature. Given this, as well as the reliance the
Fed has developed on the primary dealers to execute many of
its policies, any efforts the Fed makes toward general economic
policy are likely to disproportionately benefit financial firms.
Equally important, the Fed's monetary policy work is associated with, and depends upon, a distinct internal culture, one in
which there is an overriding imperative to avoid financial risk
and limit political conflict. As we witnessed in 2020, this suggests that the Fed is likely to be highly cautious in disbursing
government aid outside of the financial system.

This problem is exacerbated by a competence gap. Fed
staff are not trained in evaluating the credit risk posed by businesses, nonprofits, and municipalities. In 2020, the Fed avoided
holding a portfolio of nonperforming debt and stranded assets
by adopting tight terms. This restraint may have prevented Fed
loans from getting where they were most needed; with less than
$30 billion in support, the Fed was not able to avert the financial
pressures facing many smaller business and local governments,
at least not directly.

Mixing monetary and nonmonetary functions together in
one agency—creating a "kludge"—also threatens to interfere

132   with the Fed's ability to perform its primary work: keeping the economy supplied with the appropriate amount of money. Agencies with multiple, unrelated, or potentially conflicting tasks are likely to perform each of them less effectively. Real economy lending, for example, entangles the Fed with the executive branch. The Federal Reserve Act requires the Fed to seek approval from the Treasury Secretary to lend to non-banks, which it did for each of its CARES Act lending programs. And, in 2020, the Treasury Secretary agreed only to high penalty interest rates for many borrowers, limiting take-up, especially among smaller businesses and local governments. As one former central banker warns, if executive branch officials hold formal levers over some areas of central bank policy, they will be "sorely tempted to use them as informal bargaining chips over monetary policy. That's just how the world works."

The Fed's nonmonetary responsibilities also threaten to undermine its neutrality. The statutory framework governing the Fed's monetary mission is constructed to limit the Fed's ability to favor particular economic sectors or groups in managing the money supply. It is designed to treat all asset classes the same under rules set by Congress. But the Fed's credit support activities are nonneutral: they entail difficult distributive choices likely to embroil the Fed in political disputes.[*] The Fed's

---

[*] We saw a preview of this in 2020. Following the presidential election in November, the outgoing Treasury Secretary declined to authorize the Fed to continue operating most of the credit facilities beyond December 31 and requested that the Fed return the unneeded balance of the Treasury's equity investments. See Jeanna Smialek and Alan Rappeport, "Mnuchin to End Key Fed Emergency Programs, Limiting Biden," *New York Times* (November 19, 2020). Thereafter, Congress rescinded the unobligated balances made

QE programs face a similar challenge: asset purchases affect relative prices and make some projects more attractive and cheaper to finance. People holding assets that the Fed is buying (or offering to buy) experience a wealth effect, which results from the new source of demand for those assets, and improved liquidity in secondary markets for those assets. These wealth effects can be large and happen quickly. For example, markets rose substantially in 2020 in response to the news that the Fed would buy corporate credit at market prices. And they persist. Once a government agency makes investments, the government has a vested interest in the survival of the issuers in which it has invested, and so markets tend to expect the government to make further investments if needed. The government also signals to market participants that it is willing and able, at least in certain circumstances, to support certain types of issuers.

Credit programs also generate problematic lobbying pressure, for which there are not currently adequate mechanisms to monitor. For example, lobbying may have prompted the Fed to expand access to Main Street loans by raising the qualifying size caps from $2.5 billion in annual revenues to $5 billion, dropping its prohibition on using loans to refinance existing debt, and raising the maximum loan size from $150 million to $300 million. Lobbying may also have led the Fed to reduce a

available under the CARES Act to invest in Fed facilities, see Consolidated Appropriations Act, 2021, Pub. L. 116-260 (2020), § 1003(a)(1); barred the Fed from modifying the terms and conditions of those facilities in which the Treasury Secretary invested CARES Act funds, (§ 1005); and prohibited the Treasury Secretary from drawing on money from the Exchange Stabilization Fund to invest in facilities "the same as" the ones the Secretary invested CARES Act funds in, except the Term Asset-Backed Securities Loan Facility.

134   limit on how indebted a company could be before taking out a Main Street loan.

Finally, the Fed's post-2008 programs result in a much bigger balance sheet. Prior to 2008, the Fed could administer the banking system while rarely running its printing press. Its balance sheet was largely a passive instrument: its size was almost entirely determined by the public's demand for physical cash. Because the Fed can simply adjust reserve requirements or other policy variables, it generally did not need to add many more reserves to the banking system or lend to banks to ease monetary conditions. And just having the Discount Window in place helped to prevent runs on banks.

By contrast, many of the Fed's lending programs for ordinary businesses require volume to be effective. Unlike success as a monetary authority, where a job well done involves no lending at all, success as an emergency national investment authority is generally not measured by the loans that do not get made, but by those that do. For example, for the Main Street program to work, the Fed must send dollars out the door to businesses and nonprofits. There is a substantial risk that this sort of lending will politicize the Fed and change how the public views its decisions. The result may be a more polarized appointments process—as we have seen with the courts.

Distributive Equality

Even where the Fed's efforts to conduct a more general economic policy are successful, they are likely to increase inequality, given its available levers. Most obviously, backstopping shadow banking leads to more shadow banking, which likely entails more rent extraction as shadow banks privatize the gains from government-backed money creation. Shadow banking also contributes to the financialization of the economy. The financial sector (including insurance and real estate) grew from 15 percent of the economy in 1975 to 20 percent in 2007. In the last quarter of 2020, it accounted for 22 percent. Financial sector profits as a share of total corporate profits, meanwhile, grew from less than 10 percent in 1950 to 30 percent in 2005. In 2020, the percentage was still almost 25 percent.

But the problem extends beyond shadow banking. The Fed's asset purchases, for example, structurally benefit financial firms in most if not all cases, and many policy responses, like direct payments to ordinary households, are legally unavailable. The Fed simply cannot distribute money democratically in the way that Congress can. As a result, relying on the Fed as the primary macroeconomic policymaker means that the methods by which we prevent recessions disproportionately skew benefits toward the already well off. This is true even in normal times, since even conventional monetary policy works through financial institutions, stimulating the economy by lowering their cost of funding, so that they can extend more credit to ordinary borrowers.

These structural problems were on display in 2020. The Fed's efforts skewed toward lubricating capital markets by acting as a buyer of last resort to absorb tail risk that would otherwise be borne by dealers and other market participants. Moreover, because the Fed's Main Street and municipal lending facilities charged penalty interest rates, they extended little credit. Ultimately, the Fed added over $3 trillion in ways that directly

136   benefited financial firms and foreign central banks while lending less than $40 billion, or 1.3% as much, directly to support businesses and municipalities. Meanwhile, the Fed's QE program inherently favored those who owned assets over those who did not. And the Fed's decision to purchase mortgage-backed securities directly favored those who own homes in particular. When compared with a legislative stimulus such as the American Rescue Plan, Fed-led macroeconomic policy leaves a lot to be desired.*

Pressure for the Fed to pursue additional progressive goals has been predictably rebuffed. The Fed has limited its engagement on climate change to what it must do to comply with its monetary stability mandate (ensuring the banking system doesn't run out of loss-absorbing equity capital by taking correlated risks). And it has backed away from its CARES Act lending programs after the acute phase of the pandemic emergency subsided. Meanwhile, Republican members of Congress have indicated that while they will not ask questions when the

---

* A recent Parliamentary study in the UK concluded that "the evidence shows [that central bank QE programs have] had limited impact on growth and aggregate demand over the last decade." The committee further noted that while QE "is particularly effective as a tool to stabilise financial markets," "to stimulate economic growth and aggregate demand, quantitative easing is reliant on a series of transmission mechanisms that operate primarily in and through financial markets" and "[t]here is limited evidence to suggest that these [mechanisms] increase bank lending or investment, or boost consumer spending by wealthy asset holders." *Quantitative Easing: A Dangerous Addiction?* House of Lords, Economic Affairs Committee (July 16, 2021), p. 19. The empirical evidence as surveyed by academics paints a mixed picture. See Brian Fabo, Martina Jan Oková, Elizabeth Kempf, and Uboš Pástor, "Fifty Shades of QE: Comparing Findings of Central Banks and Academics," NBER Working Paper No. 27,849 (2021).

Fed stretches its statutory framework to stabilize shadow banks,
they will push back if the Fed pursues policies that challenge
business interests, such as measures to combat climate change.

Legitimacy

A more fundamental question looms. Even assuming that the
Fed could come up with effective, welfare-enhancing policies,
like a program to buy green bonds, do we want the Fed taking
on this task? As the economist Thomas Piketty argues, central
banks "lack the democratic legitimacy to venture too far beyond
their narrow sphere of expertise in banking and finance." Decisions about the purposes to which society should devote its
resources, as well as the relative priority given to various projects, are better made by elected officials than by the Fed.

Elected officials can and must delegate some decision
making to agency technocrats like those at the Fed. Indeed,
the ability to make such delegations is a critical piece of democratic self-government. As Paul Tucker argues, "The inability
to make trusted promises is the ultimate transaction cost in
public policy making"—democratic legislatures enhance their
ability to achieve public goals by enlisting technocrats as a commitment device. But there has to be a monitorable objective and
a body of technical knowledge that society recognizes as relevant to delivering on the public's goal. Hoping that the Fed will
address economic challenges we have not yet figured out how
to solve is akin in many ways to expecting the Supreme Court
to address our social and political problems. Every now and
then, we may get a big win, but, overall, the Fed is likely to be
an agent for certain elite viewpoints. That is the nature of such
organizations.

138   **Democracy and Politics**

The Fed Unbound can even be *anti-democratic*, in that it can undermine the proper functioning of our democratic institutions. Piling too many tasks into one government body, and in particular a body that has the power to create money, risks short-circuiting the legislative process. Over time, the more Congress relies upon unappropriated dollars to advance government priorities, the less likely that it will legislate solutions of its own. It is easier for legislators to rely on the Fed. But every time the Fed acts to execute on a task, the less likely it becomes that Congress will act.

This is a problem because, when it comes to macroeconomic policy, although central banks tend to operate more smoothly than the political branches, central bank action is a poor substitute for legislative action. Again, to quote Tucker:

> Elected politicians should not be able, in effect, to delegate fiscal policy to the central bank simply because they cannot agree or act themselves. Absent that stricture, we would all too likely find ourselves in an equilibrium where elected representatives leave the heavy lifting to the central bank. Arguably that has happened on both sides of the Atlantic. . . . The more central banks can do, the less the elected fiscal authority will be incentivized to do, creating a tension with our deepest political values.

As Tucker suggests, for most of the last decade, Congress failed to provide appropriate fiscal stimulus. And even though, in late December 2020 and early 2021, Congress finally legislated effectively to address macroeconomic weaknesses, it remains to be seen whether more legislative progress can be made in the 139 face of loose financial conditions facilitated by QE. In this way, Fed expansion on the asset-hand side of its balance sheet may crowd out needed legislative action by benefiting certain groups like homeowners who would otherwise lobby elected officials for economic legislation. With Fed-led macroeconomic policy tailor-made to advance their interests, why would asset owners seek other responses from Congress?

Finding a
Way Forward

As we've just examined, the Fed today holds together a fragile network of banks and shadow banks, conducting macroeconomic policy in ways that unavoidably skew benefits to asset owners and the financial sector. But given the institutional backdrop against which the Fed is operating, merely limiting the Fed's scope would almost certainly be a mistake, and possibly even result in disaster. How, then, should we proceed? To fix central banking, I believe that Congress should attend to the root of the problem. It should put the monetary system on a firmer, more public footing. It should also do more to directly tackle recessions, limit inflation, promote employment, and craft a healthier mix of macroeconomic tools so that other parts of the government can also contribute.

Putting Money on a More Public Footing

The first step to a more stable economy is addressing unregulated private money. At the moment, the problem is getting worse, not better. Policymakers must grapple not merely with the instruments we have discussed in this book—repos, euro-dollars, financial and asset-backed commercial paper, and money funds—but also a variety of novel instruments that have spread since 2008. In the wake of that year's government bailouts, libertarian technologists, opposed to what they saw as a corporatist marriage between High Finance and Washington, began to promote a new form of money to displace the dollar and ground a separate, fully private financial system. The cryptocurrencies at the center of this project—Bitcoin and Ether—use their own units of account. They are like foreign currency except they are not issued by a foreign government but by a decentralized network of computer users located around the world.

Because Bitcoin and Ether operate through an open-ended internet protocol, they bypass banks and central banks, finance ministries, and treasury departments. As a result, as they grow, they threaten to undermine the ability of governments to govern the economy. Even if these challenger currencies never reach their full ambition—to displace state money—partial uptake may erode the government's power to direct money creation toward public ends. Already, cryptocurrencies have undercut the role of the dollar payments system in the global economy. They have also created new ways for people to evade taxes and to finance criminal activity. And, in a twist, their cryptographic security features consume enormous amounts of energy—more than the entire economies of many countries.

But there are limits to the appeal of most cryptocurrencies in places like the United States. The dollar is generally a stable currency, and people who live in America use it to measure the relative value of the things they want and need. Crypto

142   alternatives pose a challenge to law enforcement but less so to the Fed.

There is, however, one significant exception: a type of cryptocurrency known as a stable value coin, or stablecoin for short. These "coins" are old wine in new bottles. They are an alternative form of dollar money. In the past decade, cryptocurrency entrepreneurs have started issuing stablecoins to create a new way for people to hold and transact in dollars outside of the purview of the Fed. Unlike Bitcoin, stablecoins are not decentralized: they are issued by individual companies, shadow banks. The biggest issuers are Tether Limited and Circle, which collectively have over $100 billion in coins in circulation as of November 2021. These new shadow banks have been joined by more established technology companies like Facebook, which announced plans to launch, in conjunction with a group of other corporations, its own digital dollar-denominated money product. Facebook initially called its coin Libra; recently, it has rebranded it under the name Diem.

Like repos and eurodollars, Tether's stablecoins and many others are (or will be) issued by firms without bank charters. But unlike repos and eurodollars, these new deposit alternatives will be primarily retail products. And as they grow, and current practices are displaced by more aggressive strategies, as seems likely, these new forms of private money may threaten to trigger runs among members of the ordinary public.

There is a relatively straightforward way, however, to solve this problem. Both "traditional" shadow banking, the sort that revolves around Wall Street firms and has developed over the past half century, and the "new" shadow banking, the sort associated with Silicon Valley and cryptographic technology, can be

tackled using a set of tools that are standard in other areas of law   143
and regulation. The foundation of securities law, for example, is
a functional definition of a "security." Insurance law works the
same way. Anyone creating products that function as securities
or insurance is subject to the relevant regulatory regime.

As the legal scholar Morgan Ricks has persuasively argued,
we currently lack such a foundation for money and banking
law. Congress should fix this by ensuring that any firm issuing
deposits or their equivalent is required to obtain a bank charter.
Firms that are already engaging in banking activities yet outside
the Fed's regulatory perimeter could be given an opportunity to
transition. This might mean that these firms divest nonbanking
businesses and reduce leverage. Or it might mean they cease to
issue alternative forms of money and exit the banking business.
Broker dealers, for example, might "term" out their funding,
meaning they would cease to use overnight repos to finance
their asset portfolios and, instead, raise money from long-term
investors. Digital dollar wallet providers, meanwhile, could
continue offering dollar accounts to their customers but start
backing them 1:1 with deposits held by a chartered bank rather
than using their customers' funds to invest in risky assets.

In addition to enforcing the regulatory perimeter so that
privately owned money issuers are subject to public direction
and oversight, Congress might also create a new public option
for money. For nearly a century, Americans have used physical
currency issued by the Fed. But they have been limited to using
deposits (and their online equivalent) issued by investor-owned
and -operated banks. Congress could expand the options available to Americans, potentially crowding out some dangerous
forms of private money, by authorizing the Fed to issue deposit

144   money directly. Along with coauthors, I have termed such money FedAccounts: basic bank account balances with no fees, which can be transferred instantly and are nondefaultable. Fed-Accounts are a type of "central bank digital currency," or CBDC.*

They would offer a way for the government to rectify predatory and exclusionary practices in the investor-owned banking system that have significantly harmed low-income and minority communities by making it hard (if not impossible) for many households to open and maintain bank accounts.

There is also a way for state governments to complement such efforts. States have the power to charter banks and could issue charters for publicly owned banks sometimes referred to as public banks. Public banks would be like investor-owned banks but controlled by executives pursuing public policy aims, such as infrastructure investment, access to credit for underserved communities, and low-cost basic financial services. These public banks could extend credit alongside investor-owned banks and join the banking system that the Fed is already charged with administering. Among other things, they could be designed to redress the failure of the investor-owned banking system to adequately assist low-income and minority borrowers, a failure that has prevented millions of households from building wealth over generations. Congress could also charter public banks, seeding new organizations to pursue various federal priorities. Such national investment authorities could operate more

---

* CBDCs are increasingly being developed and deployed by other countries. For example, China launched a CBDC denominated in its currency, the yuan, in 2020. Already this electronic yuan or eCNY is being used in several cities, and the country's leaders plan to take it global in the coming years. The Bahamas also recently began issuing the "Sand Dollar," a CBDC that helps low-income households access the digital payments economy.

effective alternatives to the Fed's Main Street lending programs, for example. They could also be designed to offer credit to state and local governments.

A more dramatic reform, last seriously considered in the 1930s, would be for the government to take back its money monopoly entirely. This would mean direct issue, in which Congress or other government agencies set monetary policy by issuing all the money the economy needs. Under this approach, Congress would allow banks and shadow banks to continue operating but require them to backstop all of their short-term liabilities with government-issued money. This is called full-reserve or "narrow" banking. It would also stabilize our financial system but is not necessary to achieve that goal and would require a more fundamental reworking of current law (which, as we've seen in chapters 2 and 3, revolves around monetary outsourcing).

Creating a Healthier Macroeconomic Policy Mix

Enforcing the regulatory perimeter for banking and putting the monetary system on a more public footing would reduce or eliminate the Fed's need to use ad hoc lending and purchasing programs. It would also improve the stability, efficacy, and fairness of our financial system. But we can do more to achieve a stronger economic architecture by creating new ways to combat recessions and address inflationary booms so that the Fed has less reason to stretch its monetary tools to tackle these problems. After all, many macroeconomic troubles have little to do with the money supply and could much more effectively and equitably be resolved using other means. The end goal should be a Fed engaged in fine-tuning, ensuring that a lack of money

146   is not the reason that the economy shrinks and that a surfeit of
money is not the reason prices jump higher.

There are a variety of ways that Congress might make it
easier for the Fed to continue its role as our country's money
manager while avoiding the circumstances that give rise to programs like QE. On the fiscal side, Congress can create new "automatic stabilizers." These are legislative programs that increase
government outlays during economic downturns and reduce
them during economic recoveries without requiring additional
congressional action. Perhaps the most important automatic
stabilizer today is the federal unemployment insurance program, which replaces lost wages when people lose their jobs.
Unemployment insurance boosts economic activity when the
private sector reduces its spending and therefore increases the
likelihood that the economy will grow at full potential.

One promising idea would be to authorize the Treasury
to distribute payments to low- and moderate-income households whenever the three-month average unemployment rate
increases at least 0.50 percentage points relative to its low over
the previous year. Under this plan, developed by the economist Claudia Sahm, checks would automatically go out from the
Treasury Department to qualifying households during downturns.* The legal scholar Yair Listokin has also outlined a series

* The past two years have demonstrated just how effective such a program
could be in rapidly increasing wages and employment, with Congress
authorizing onetime stimulus payments in March 2020 as part of the
CARES Act, in December 2020 as part of an omnibus spending package,
and again in March 2021 as part of Biden's American Rescue Plan. These
packages sped an economic recovery that would have taken far longer if
Congress had left it primarily to central bankers.

of legal remedies to recessions, including countercyclical utility regulatory policy, student loan forgiveness, and modifications to the bankruptcy code. Related policy options include promoting shovel-ready infrastructure projects, buttressing state and local government budgets during downturns, suspending evictions and foreclosures, and offering out of work people public service jobs. Unlike monetary policy, such programs would stimulate demand, counteract disinflationary tendencies, and drive up employment without directly enriching asset owners or aiding the financial sector.

There are also ways to check inflation that do not involve monetary policy. For example, officials can address healthcare inflation through further reforms to government healthcare programs and greater investment in healthcare services. Officials can address climbing house prices through new zoning policies and federal investment in low-income housing. Officials can use industrial policy to target bottlenecks, directing resources toward expanding capacity in key sectors. And officials can use antitrust enforcement to tackle price markups in highly concentrated industries. When inflation is the result of supply-side constraints, as opposed to excess money printing, these measures are far more effective and equitable than monetary tightening, which dampens activity across the economy.

It is also important for Congress to play a bigger role in managing the economy and not rely too heavily on independent administrators or the executive branch. Even in our fractured political present, Congress has proven itself to be the most effective institution for developing tailored responses to economic shocks that advance the interests of ordinary households

148   and businesses. When compared to central banking and other
        forms of expert administration, democratic politics is messy,
        and congressional enactments are bound to involve compro-
        mises. But legislators are more accountable to voters than tech-
        nocrats, and this shows in the laws they pass, which tend to be
        more egalitarian. The major packages we've seen since 2020 are
        prime examples.

        Automatic stabilizers, supply-side management, and a
        more active Congress would not, of course, render central banks
        obsolete. We would still need the Fed to manage money and
        administer the banking system. But the Fed's job would be sim-
        pler and more appropriately addressed using the tools it already
        has. And the financial sector would occupy a much smaller role
        in our government's efforts to combat recessions. Most impor-
        tantly, by adding these other mechanisms to the policy mix,
        Congress could foster a stronger economy while ensuring that
        the benefits of economic growth flow more evenly across Amer-
        ican society.

        Our system of money and banking is legally constructed. Every-
        thing from the definition of the monetary unit to the system for
        issuing ledger entries is a function of government policy. Over
        the past seventy years, a shadow banking system has developed.
        Since 2008, the Fed has repeatedly backstopped this system
        through large-scale lending and purchasing programs. This
        institutional architecture has certain distributional conse-
        quences: it expands the financial sector, it facilitates speculative
        trading, and it enriches asset owners. But there is nothing nat-
        ural or inevitable about it. The choice to maintain this system is

a political one. Just as our government built these institutions
and structured these delegations, it can rebuild them or change
them. My hope is that by better understanding what is at stake
in the design of our monetary order, we can have a richer democratic discourse about what comes next.

This book would not have been possible without my teachers, the many incredible people who taught me to ask questions, seek answers, and try to connect the dots. I would like to specially acknowledge a few of these teachers for the contributions they made—directly or indirectly—to this particular project. First and foremost, I am grateful to Morgan Ricks. When I read Morgan's book, *The Money Problem*, I discovered how Archimedes must have felt when he took his famous bath. Few books change how you think about the world; Morgan's did. In the years since, Morgan has also helped me immeasurably, including reading several drafts of this manuscript. It is no exaggeration to say that this book would not have been possible without him.

The basis for this project dates to my years as a student. In law school, David Grewal deepened my understanding of the relationship between markets and the state, always investing in my work as if it were his own and always making it better. Robert Post showed me how to think about law and how law works at its best. Jon Macey taught me always to be skeptical and encouraged my curiosity for all things banking. In college, Richard Tuck, Emma Rothschild, Ben Friedman, and Stephen Marglin turned me on to money, politics, and economics, and offered me a conceptual framework for thinking about their relationship to each other.

Outside of school, I had the extraordinary privilege to grapple firsthand with some of the problems this book examines while working at the Federal Reserve Bank of New York, US Treasury Department, and Biden-Harris Transition. I learned

so much from the many dedicated public servants I met during
those years.

Since reaching the other side of the lectern, I've continued
to learn about banking, central banking, and public administration from my many brilliant colleagues in the academy. I owe a
special thanks to Chris Desan, Jeff Gordon, and Dan Tarullo—
three amazing people and exceptional scholars. Chris's work
on English monetary history inspired and informed my work
on American banking, including this project. Jeff's ener-
getic investment in my research has added critical nuance
throughout. Dan's unparalleled understanding of contemporary central banking, deep-seated commitment to the public
interest, and preternatural patience immeasurably improved my
analysis of many of the questions examined here and allowed
me to avoid many, if not all, of the oversights and mistakes that
it is the job of academics to steadily weed out of their work.

For invaluable assistance crafting the argument and navi-
gating the past year, I would like to thank Ash Ahmed. For brilliant aide with revising the manuscript, I owe a debt to James
Brandt, Gary Gensler, Daniel Herz-Roiphe, Kate Judge, Anna
Kovner, Nick Lemann, Yair Listokin, Emily Menand, Louis
Menand, Katharina Pistor, Parth Sheth, and Jimmy So. For
generous help at various points on the book and related work,
thank you to Dan Awrey, Pierpaolo Barbieri, Michael Barr, Pat-
rick Bolton, Erik Gerding, David Grewal, Adrienne Harris, Bob
Hockett, Aziz Huq, Amy Kapczynski, Robert Katzmann, Jeremy
Kessler, Jeremy Kress, Simon Johnson, Kate Judge, Da Lin, Yair
Listokin, Jon Macey, Jane Manners, Jamie McAndrews, Gil-
lian Metzger, Henry Monaghan, Saule Omarova, Nick Parrillo,

152 Katharina Pistor, Robert Post, Dave Pozen, Jed Purdy, Jed Rakoff, Sarah Bloom Raskin, Noah Rosenblum, George Selgin, Ganesh Sitaraman, Joe Sommer, Eric Talley, Paul Tucker, and Art Wilmarth. Thank you also to Gillian Lester and Columbia Law School, where I have been blessed to be able to teach and write for the past three years; Camille McDuffie and everyone at Columbia Global Reports; and Nick Lemann, for envisioning and championing this project.

Last, and most of all, I want to thank my family and friends. Good scholarship grows from a foundation of love and support. If I've not met that mark here, it is surely not for a lack of either. For as long as I can remember, my parents have encouraged my curiosity and creativity, in ways above and beyond the call. My brother, Joseph, has been there for me through thick and thin—steadfast, kind, and unwavering. My wife, Emily, has offered me a happiness I never imagined possible. And our daughter, Maeve—her twinkle lights my world.

For an excellent overview of central banking that takes a theoretical and historical perspective, I recommend Curzio Giannani's *The Age of Central Banks* (2011). For those interested in reading more about how central banking has changed over the past thirteen years, I recommend Perry Mehrling's *The New Lombard Street: How the Fed Became the Dealer of Last Resort* (2011). Mehrling is an economist famous for popularizing the "money view," the idea that the economy is composed of a series of obligations incurred by different actors—households, businesses, governments, nonprofits—that these actors discharge over time using money instruments like deposits. On the money view, the critical question is whether economic actors can meet their obligations as they come due each day. Banks play a special role because they are a source of money: they offer actors a way to escape this "survival constraint" when their cash flows turn negative. Central banks are even more special because they serve this same function for banks, keeping the entire system running. In his book, Mehrling looks at how the Fed has adapted to a world dominated by shadow banks.

Mehrling's book, which takes shadow banking as a given, is technical and conceptual. For a thick descriptive account of the politics and economics of contemporary central banking, two books about the recent crises by Adam Tooze are a good place to turn. In a 2018 volume, *Crashed: How a Decade of Financial Crises Changed the World,* Tooze shows how the 2008 panic was a global crisis because the dollar is a global currency with financial firms creating dollar money claims all over the world (especially Europe). In *Shutdown: How Covid Shook the World's*

154   *Economy* (2021), Tooze extends the story, recounting how cen-
      tral banks reprised their playbooks from 2008 to combat
      another run on the shadow banking system.[*]

      For those interested in a critical examination of whether
central banks as institutions are up to the tasks they are now tack-
ling, I recommend Sir Paul Tucker's magnum opus *Unelected
Power: The Quest for Legitimacy in Central Banking and the Regulatory State* (2018). Tucker was Deputy Governor of the Bank
of England from 2009 to 2013 and offers both a critique of the
expanding activities of central banks and a program for reform.
Another critique and program for reform can be found in Yair
Listokin's pathbreaking book *Law and Macroeconomics: Legal
Remedies to Recessions* (2019). Listokin, a legal scholar and economist, offers a range of compelling ways for the government to
promote broad-based economic growth while reducing our reliance on unconventional central bank policies.

      Of course, as I've argued here, it is impossible to understand
contemporary central banking without understanding banking
and shadow banking. The best book on shadow banking—why it
threatens the stability of our economic and financial system and
what to do about it—is *The Money Problem: Rethinking Financial
Regulation* (2016) by Morgan Ricks. Ricks offers the definitive
account of the 2008 crisis and a masterful assessment of the
deficiencies in the post-2008 regulatory framework.

      For a longer view of American banking, I recommend Bray
Hammond's *Banking and Politics in America: From the Revolution*

---

[*] For another excellent resource that offers ongoing and cutting-edge analysis
of today's monetary-financial system and the Fed's role in it, see Nathan
Tankus's newsletter, *Notes on the Crises*, available online.

to the Civil War (1957). I also recommend the excellent 1973
volume by the great legal historian James Willard Hurst, *A Legal
History of Money*, which offers a more technical overview of similar terrain and brings the story up to the point when the New
Deal order began to fray. For a terrific and insightful treatment
of banking and central banking that examines the diversity of
thought about how to create money in America, I recommend
Susan Hoffman's *Politics and Banking: Ideas, Public Policy, and
the Creation of Financial Institutions* (2001).

Finally, if you want to go even deeper to understand the intel-
lectual, historical, and legal foundations of modern banking,
shadow banking, and central banking, the book to read is Chris
Desan's monumental *Making Money: Coins, Currency, and the
Coming of Capitalism* (2014). Desan's account of the rise of banks
and central banks as institutions for expanding the money supply
and sweeping overview of how the English monetary system
evolved over the past millennium helps illuminate why we should
be concerned that our economy today depends on a mass of
investor-owned shadow banks backstopped on an ad hoc basis by
a powerful, politically insulated central bank.[*]

---

[*] Parts of this book draw on other work I've written. Chapter 1 on the Fed's
response to the pandemic extends an article I published in 2021 in the
Stanford Journal of Law, Business & Finance, "The Federal Reserve and the
2020 Economic and Financial Crisis." Chapter 2 builds on a framework I
outlined for thinking about the structure and purpose of American banking
law in "Why Supervise Banks? The Foundations of the American Monetary
Settlement," published in 2021 in the *Vanderbilt Law Review*. Other parts,
especially chapters 3 and 4, draw on a not-yet-published work about the
Federal Reserve, "Administering the Banking System: The Logic and Limits
of the Federal Reserve Act."

PREFACE

12 **They lost nearly all of their investors' money:** *Financial Crisis Inquiry Commission, Final Report* (2011), pp. 240–42.

12 **by far the most of any bankrupt company in history:** *Financial Crisis Inquiry Commission, Final Report*, pp. 339–40. By 2010, an even more astounding $873 billion of claims would emerge against the failed investment house. As a point of comparison, just fifteen years prior to Lehman's collapse, the largest financial institution in the US, Citibank, a government-chartered bank, had around $160 billion in liabilities. *Citicorp, Annual Report Pursuant to Section 13 or 15(d) of the Securities Exchange Act of 1934 for the Fiscal Year Ended December 31, 1996* (1997), p. 26 (listing the bank's total deposits and long-term debt for year-end 1993).

13 **reached the end of a "Second Gilded Age":** William D. Cohan, *House of Cards: A Tale of Hubris and Wretched Excess on Wall Street* (2010), p. 319.

14 **Bank of Japan holds assets worth over 700 trillion yen:** Since WWII, the size of the Bank of Japan's balance sheet was driven primarily by demand for paper money and hovered steadily below 10 percent of annual economic output. Masato Shizume, "The Historical Evolution of Monetary Policy (Goals and Instruments) in Japan: From the Central Bank of an Emerging Economy to the Central Bank of a Mature Economy," in Stefano Battilossi, Youssef Cassis & Kazuhiko Yago, eds., *Handbook of the History of Money and Currency* (2020), pp. 927, 949. As of May 2021, the bank's balance sheet stood at approximately 130 percent of annual economic output. "BOJ Data Shows Assets Quadruple to $6.5 Under Kuroda's Aggressive Easing," Kyodo News (May 27, 2021).

14 **The European Central Bank:** As historian Adam Tooze put it, "the ECB [European Central Bank] is the only agency [in Europe] engaged in economic policy worthy of the name." "The Death of the Central Bank Myth," *Foreign Policy* (May 13, 2020).

INTRODUCTION

16 **"but in consequence of appropriations made by law":** US Constitution, Art I, § 9, Cl. 7.

18 **he had no idea the Fed even had the authority:** "Barney Frank: Ownership Issue Key to Recouping AIG Bonuses," *American Morning*, CNN, March 18, 2009.

18 **where was the Fed planning to get $80 billion:** Neil Irwin, *The Alchemists: Three Central Bankers and a World on Fire*, ch. 11 (2013).

19   so that these institutions could backstop financial businesses in Europe and Asia: Adam Tooze, *Crashed: How A Decade of Financial Crises Changed the World* (2018).

20   financial markets cracked up: See generally Gara Afonso, Marco Cipriani, Adam Copeland, Anna Kovner, Gabriele La Spada, and Antoine Martin, "The Market Events of Mid-September 2019," *Economic Policy Review* 27, no. 2 (2021); Nathan Tankus, "Looking Back at 'Repo Madness' One Year Later," Notes on the Crises (September 21, 2020).

21   smaller than it was projected to be before the pandemic: Mitchell Barnes, Lauren Bauer, and Wendy Edelberg, "11 Facts on the Economic Recovery From the COVID-19 Pandemic," Brookings (September 2021), p. 4 (showing gap between actual GDP in 2021:Q2 and GDP for that quarter as projected in January 2020).

22   surely, these advocates argue: See, for example, Network for Greening the Financial System, Adapting Central Bank Operations to a Hotter World: Reviewing Some Options (March 2021); Adam Tooze, "Why Central Banks Need to Step Up on Global Warming," *Foreign Policy* (July 20, 2019); Kim Stanley Robinson, "A Climate Plan for a World in Flames," *Financial Times* (August 20, 2021); Mark

Blyth & Eric Lonergan, "Print Less but Transfer More: Why Central Banks Should Give Money Directly to the People," 93 *Foreign Affairs* 98 (2014); Robert Hockett, "Spread the Fed: From Federal Disintegration Through Community QE to Central Bank Decentralization," *LPE Blog* (August 12, 2020); Robert Hockett, "The Fed Is a 'Development Bank'—Make It Our Development Bank Again," *Forbes* (September 30, 2020).

CHAPTER ONE

31   but no Canadian financial institutions failed: Stephen Gordon, "Recession of 2008–09 in Canada," *The Canadian Encyclopedia* (2021). The Canadian economy *did* experience a retraction in 2009 as a result of the recession suffered by its major trading partners, especially the United States, and the collapse in oil prices. But, with its financial system intact, Canada was able to bounce back quickly: Canadian employment fell less than 2.5 percent from its pre-crisis peak and recovered that level by January 2011. US employment, by contrast, fell 6 percent and took until May 2014 to recover.

32   has been caused by a particular type of structural vulnerability: See Hugh Rockoff, "It Is Always the Shadow Banks: The Regulatory Status of the Banks That Failed and Ignited America's Greatest Financial Panics," in

158   Hugh Rockoff and Isao Suto, eds., *Coping with Financial Crises* (2018), pp. 77–106; Morgan Ricks, *The Money Problem: Rethinking Financial Regulation* (2016), pp. 78–142. These panics are also the primary source of the great macroeconomic disasters in US history. Morgan Ricks, *The Money Problem*, pp. 102–42. For an economic analysis of the Great Recession in particular, see Ben S. Bernanke, "The Real Effects of the Financial Crisis," Brookings Papers on Economic Activity, September 13–14, 2008 (finding that the unusual severity of the Great Recession was due primarily to the panic in funding and securitization markets, which disrupted the supply of credit).

33   **also function as a substitute for cash:** Geoff Miller and Jon Macey call them "nondeposit deposits." Jonathan R. Macey and Geoffrey P. Miller, "Nondeposit Deposits and the Future of Bank Regulation," *Michigan Law Review* 91 (1992).

34   **the system in which private firms supply most of the money in the economy starts to fall apart:** Morgan Ricks, *The Money Problem*, pp. 1–106.

35   **solved the problems that had triggered the global financial crisis:** See, e.g., Jerome H. Powell, "Relationship Between Regulation and Economic Growth," Testimony Before the Committee on Banking, Housing, and Urban Affairs, US Senate (June 22, 2017); Randal K. Quarles, "Early Observations on Improving the Effectiveness of Post-Crisis Regulation," American Bar Association Banking Law Committee Annual Meeting (January 19, 2018).

35   **thought that the government had actually overcorrected:** See, e.g., Lalita Clozel, "Fed to Further Overhaul Stress-Testing Regime, Making It Easier for Banks to Pass," *Wall Street Journal* (November 9, 2018).

35   **twenty-four Wall Street firms known as "the primary dealers":** Federal Reserve Bank of New York, List of Primary Dealers, www.newyorkfed.org/markets /primarydealers.

38   **The Fed would structure these loans as "swaps":** Federal Reserve, Press Release, Coordinated Central Bank Action to Enhance the Provision of U.S. Dollar Liquidity (March 15, 2020).

28   **consider some transaction-level data:** Data available online at Federal Reserve Bank of New York, Central Bank Liquidity Swap Operations, www.newyorkfed.org /markets/desk-operations/central -bank-liquidity-swap-operations.

41   **its assets stopped being worth $1 per share:** *Financial Crisis Inquiry Commission, Final Report* (2011), p. 356.

41 **fears that falling asset prices might cause money funds to break the buck:** *Federal Reserve, Financial Stability Report* (May 2020), p. 13 (Figure B).

41 **quickly stepped in to help them out:** Tim McLaughlin, "Exclusive: Goldman Injects $1 Billion into Own Money-Market Funds After Heavy Withdrawals," Reuters (March 21, 2021).

42 **The biggest issuers:** Lance Pan, Cap. Advisors Grp., *A Decade of the Commercial Paper Market and Its Role in Institutional Liquidity Portfolios* (2018), p. 6 (listing the top five issuers as Toronto Dominion Bank, Toyota Motor Credit Corporation, ING Financial Services, JPMorgan Chase, and National Australia Bank).

43 **Amid the turmoil, Secretary Steven Mnuchin drew on the account:** See Lev Menand, "The Federal Reserve and the 2020 Economic and Financial Crisis," *Stanford Journal of Law, Business & Finance* 26 (2021), pp. 295, 330–32.

44 **backstop financial firms in the money claim business:** Commentators sometimes say there was a "dash for cash"—and this is true but only in a sense. It is not that in March 2020 a bunch of people suddenly decided they wanted to hold a lot more money and less of other forms of assets like stocks, bonds, and real estate. Nor was it that foreign firms suddenly decided they wanted to hold more US dollars and less euros or yen. Financial and nonfinancial businesses at home and abroad already held a type of dollar denominated money: deposit alternatives issued by shadow banks. They "dashed" from one type of dollar money (repos, eurodollars, money market funds, commercial paper) to another, the deposits issued by government-chartered banks.

44 **nineteenth-century financial market champion:** Walter Bagehot, *Lombard Street: A Description of the Money Market* (1873), p. 51.

45 **doubling in a matter of days:** Market Yield on U.S. Treasury Securities at 10-Year Constant Maturity, FRED, https://fred .stlouisfed.org/series/DGS10.

45 **liquidity in Treasury markets dried up:** Lorie K. Logan, "Treasury Market Liquidity and Early Lessons from the Pandemic Shock," Remarks at Brookings-Chicago Booth Task Force on Financial Stability Meeting (October 23, 2020).

46 **they were thus forced to sell these investments at whatever the price:** Lorie K. Logan, "The Federal Reserve's Market Functioning Purchases: From Supporting to Sustaining," Remarks at SIFMA Webinar (July 15, 2020); Carolyn Sissoko, "A Fire Sale in the US Treasury Market: What the

160   Coronavirus Crisis Teaches Us About the Fundamental Instability of Our Current Financial Structure," *Just Money* (March 27, 2020); Alex Etra, "2020 UST March Madness," Money: Inside and Out (January 13, 2021) (identifying the key sources of selling as foreign central banks, bond funds, and hedge funds).

46   the Fed stunned commentators and market participants: Lorie K. Logan, "The Federal Reserve's Market Functioning Purchases: From Supporting to Sustaining."

48   the Fed would not "run out of ammunition": Christopher Condon, Steve Matthews, Matthew Boesler, and Rich Miller, "Fed Is 'Not Going to Run Out of Ammunition,' Powell Vows," Bloomberg (March 26, 2020).

50   The CARES Act made this possible: See Lev Menand, "The Federal Reserve and the 2020 Economic and Financial Crisis," p. 295.

52   "support[ed] credit to employers by providing liquidity to the market for outstanding corporate bonds": "Secondary Market Corporate Credit Facility," Board of Governors of the Federal Reserve System (March 23, 2020).

52   functioned as another means of supporting shadow banks: Whereas the panic prevention programs provided shadow banks with funding liquidity—they allowed eligible borrowers to shore up the liability sides of their balance sheets—the SMCCF enhanced market liquidity by serving as a buyer of last resort for certain assets. Market liquidity can be a function of funding liquidity (because runs on dealers prevent them from being able to intermediate capital markets). See, for example, Markus K. Brunnermeier and Lasse Heje Pedersen, "Market Liquidity and Funding Liquidity," *Review of Financial Studies* 22 (2009), p. 2201 (distinguishing between market liquidity and funding liquidity). But restoring market liquidity by directly acting as a dealer is different from restoring market liquidity by providing funding liquidity to dealers. The Fed was providing special treatment for a sector of the economy: capital markets.

53   it has not used this authority since 1933: See 43 Fed. Reg. 53,708 (November 11, 1978). For a comprehensive overview of the Fed's municipal bond purchases from its founding to March 31, 1932, see Municipal Warrants Purchased by Federal Reserve Banks (April 29, 1932). These purchases total $219,943,000 and are concentrated between 1915 and 1917 (in the latter year the Board told the FRBs that it was "inadvisable for them to invest . . . in [municipal] warrants") and in 1931 and 1932 (when the FRBs resumed purchasing municipal warrants in size to "accommodate member banks" under stress).

53   TALF 2.0 also increased the flow of credit: As Ben Bernanke explained of TALF 1.0, the program "substitute[s] public for private balance sheet capacity . . . to lower rates and [prompt] greater availability of consumer and small business credit." Ben Bernanke, Chairman, Federal Reserve, Stamp Lecture at the London School of Economics: The Crisis and the Policy Response (January 13, 2009).

54   its creditors received only between fourteen and seventy-five cents on the dollar: Matthew Dolan, "Judge Approves Detroit's Bankruptcy-Exit Plan," *Wall Street Journal* (November 7, 2014).

54   why the Municipal Liquidity Facility set such high interest rates: The Fed's "Regulation A" currently requires the Federal Reserve Banks to charge penalty rates. See 12 C.F.R. § 201.4(c)(7)(ii) (2020) (requiring that the Board set rates "at a penalty level" that is at "a premium to the market rate in normal circumstances[,] . . . [e]ncourages repayment, and discourages use . . . as . . . economic conditions normalize"). The Board self-imposed this requirement in 2015. 80 Fed. Reg. 78,960 (December 18, 2015) (codified at 12 C.F.R § 201.4(c)(7)(ii)). Section 14(d) of the FRA empowers

the Board to establish "rates of discount," including rates on 13(3) loans, to accommodate commerce and business at whatever levels it deems appropriate. See 12 U.S.C. § 357; see also *Raichle v. Fed. Rsrv. Bank of N.Y.*, 34 F.2d 910, 915 (2d Cir. 1929) ("It would be an unthinkable burden upon any banking system if its . . . discount rates were to be subject to judicial review").

55   municipalities benefited from the Municipal Liquidity Facility even though the Fed never bought their bonds: For a review of these benefits, see Written Testimony of Mike Konczal, "Lending in a Crisis: Reviewing the Federal Reserve's Emergency Lending Powers During the Pandemic and Examining Proposals to Address Future Economic Crises," US House of Representatives, Committee on Financial Services, Subcommittee on National Security, International Development, and Monetary Policy (September 23, 2021), pp. 3–4. See also Robert Bernhardt, Stefania D'Amico, and Santiago I. Sordo Palacios, "The Impact of the Pandemic and the Fed's Muni Program on Illinois Muni Yields," Chicago Fed Letter No. 449 (December 2020). For a contrary view, identifying those left behind by the Fed's municipal rescue program, see Max Moran, "The Fed's Municipal Lending Failed Black Public-Sector Workers," Revolving Door Project (August 19, 2021).

162

57 **take-up was relatively limited:** See Federal Reserve, www.federalreserve.gov/monetarypolicy/mainstreetlending.html. See also Nick Timiraos, "Fed Had a Loan Plan for Midsize Firms Hurt by Covid. It Found Few Takers," *Wall Street Journal* (January 4, 2021); Dion Rabouin, "Fed Programs Have Kept Finance Flowing to Fossil Fuels," *Wall Street Journal* (November 19, 2021).

58 **employing its balance sheet in ways that shape economic activity:** Saule T. Omarova, "Why We Need a National Investment Authority," *Cornell L. Sch. Legal Stud. Rsch.*, Paper No. 20-34 (2020); Robert C. Hockett and Saule T. Omarova, "Private Wealth and Public Goods: A Case for a National Investment Authority," *Journal of Corporate Law* 43 (2018), p. 437; Robert C. Hockett and Saule T. Omarova, "White Paper: A National Investment Authority," *Cornell Legal Studies*, Research Paper No. 18-10 (2018).

65 **Jeff Bezos went from being worth an estimated $114 billion:** *Forbes*, "#1 Jeff Bezos," https://www.forbes.com/profile/jeff-bezos/?sh=32a0891b2382 (last accessed November 25, 2021).

65 **Elon Musk's fortune increased from $20 billion to $190 billion over the same period:** *Forbes*, "#2 Elon Musk," https://www.forbes.com/profile/elon

-musk/?list=forbes-400&sh=42b721d77999 (last accessed November 25, 2021).

66 **US billionaires collectively saw their wealth increase:** https://inequality.org/great-divide/updates-billionaire-pandemic.

65 **Two groups took wealth share during the pandemic:** Michael Batty, Ella Deeken, and Alice Henriques Volz, "Wealth Inequality and COVID-19: Evidence from the Distributional Financial Accounts," FEDS Notes (2021).

CHAPTER TWO

69 **for-profit banks were bastions of privilege:** Gretchen Ritter, *Goldbugs and Greenbacks: The Antimonopoly Tradition and the Politics of Finance in America, 1865–1896* (2011).

70 **the American Monetary Settlement:** Lev Menand, "Why Supervise Banks? The Foundations of the American Monetary Settlement," *Vanderbilt Law Review* 74, no. 4 (2021), pp. 951–1022.

71 **This new approach to money was not without its drawbacks:** A. Andréadès, *A History of the Bank of England* (1909), pp. 75–80; Christine Desan, *Making Money: Coins, Currency, and the Coming of Capitalism*, pp. 295–329, 361–70.

71 **Congress set up a similar system in the United States:** Bray

Hammond, *Banks and Politics in America: From the Revolution to the Civil War* (1957), pp. 164–68.

71 **the English monetary system did not take to American soil:** Hezekiah Niles, "To Correct Abuses by the Bank," *Niles' Wkly. Reg.* (March 7, 1818), pp. 17, 23.

72 **the political foundations of the system collapsed:** Hammond, pp. 405–50.

73 **Congress expected that national banks would replace the patchwork of state banks:** Lev Menand and Morgan Ricks, "Federal Corporate Law and the Business of Banking," *University of Chicago Law Review* 88 (2021).

76 **roughly $1 trillion of government-issued cash circulating:** There is actually $2.2 trillion of currency in circulation, see Federal Reserve, Factors Affecting Reserve Balances of Depository Institutions and Condition Statement of Federal Reserve Banks (November 26, 2020) (Table 1), but perhaps as much as 70 percent of this is used overseas by people in other countries, see J. P. Konig, "How Much U.S. Currency is Held Overseas?" Bullionstar (July 3, 2019); Katherine Judson, "The Death of Cash? Not So Fast: Demand for U.S. Currency at Home and Abroad, 1990–2016," International Cash Conference 2017—War on Cash: Is There a Future for Cash? (April 25, 2017).

76 **banks in the US maintain nearly $18 trillion:** Federal Reserve, H.8 Assets and Liabilities of Commercial Banks in the United States (November 26, 2021) (Table 1).

77 **could the state expand the money supply beyond gold and silver:** This justification for using banks to expand the money supply and delegating control over them to private interests dates back to the 1690s. Hamilton emphasized it in his push to charter the BUS. See Alexander Hamilton, "Report on a National Bank [1790]," in *The Works of Alexander Hamilton* (1810), p. 82 (noting that direct government issuance of paper money is "liable to abuse"); p. 95 (describing danger of government-directed credit). And even the opponents of banking accepted its premise: the government should not issue money that is not collateralized by precious metals.

77 **only a state can create a framework in which the money issued by private actors:** See Christine Desan, *Making Money: Coins, Currency, and the Coming of Capitalism* (2014), pp. 38–50.

78 **might be tempted to depreciate the currency:** Alexander Hamilton, "The Report of the Secretary of the Treasury, (Alexander Hamilton), on the Subject of a National Bank," in Charles Brockden Brown and

164 Robert Walsh, *American Register, or General Repository of History, Politics, and Science* (1810), pp. 225, 238: "The stamping of paper is an operation so much easier than the laying of taxes, that a government, in the practice of paper emissions, would rarely fail in any such emergency, to indulge itself too far in the employment of that resource, to avoid as much as possible, one less auspicious to present popularity."

78 **By sharing a piece of its power:** US Treasury Secretary, *Report on the Finances* (1862), p. 16 ("Notes circulating as money . . . [form] a highly accumulative species of property").

78 **merely by spending it to pay the government's bills:** US Treasury Secretary, *Report on the Finances*, p. 17.

78 **which would "convert the treasury into a government bank":** US Treasury Secretary, *Report on the Finances*.

78 **"can perform the functions of a bank by loaning money":** Cong. Globe 1451 (February 10, 1863) (Rep. Samuel Hooper).

79 **it did not want the Bank to "oppress" the merchants and businessmen:** Bank of England Act (1694) § 26.

80 **copied Parliament's language almost verbatim:** An Act to revive the incorporation of the Bank of North America, ch. 767, § 5 (March 17, 1787), reprinted in *Laws of the Commonwealth of Pennsylvania* (1810).

80 **Banks cannot absorb all the profits of industry:** Cong. Rec., 53rd Cong., 3rd Sess., Vol. XXVI, Part IV, at 177 (January 5, 1895) (emphasis added). President Wilson echoed this line when he pushed Congress to create the Federal Reserve Board to rein in private bankers. See Woodrow Wilson, Message Regarding the Banking System, June 23, 1913.

80 **to prevent . . . "undue concentration of resources":** 12 U.S.C. § 1843(a)(2).

81 **Congress dropped its limits in the 1990s:** See Riegle-Neal Interstate Banking and Branching Efficiency Act, Pub. L. 103-328, 103d Cong., 1st Sess. (1994).

81 **remains the most diffuse in the world:** Financial Stability Oversight Council, Annual Report (2011), p. 57.

82 **"to let each in his turn enjoy an opportunity to profit by our bounty":** President Jackson's Veto Message Regarding the Bank of the United States (July 10, 1832).

82 **"the liberty of a democracy is not safe":** S. Doc. No. 173, 75th Cong., 3d Sess. 1 (1938).

82   **each bank checks the others:**
In a fiat money regime, that is. If
a country uses the gold standard,
then the bank is constrained by
its ability to redeem its notes
and deposits for gold. Of course,
even then, a bank can "suspend
convertibility" and if it is dominant
enough (and the government goes
along) it can continue circulating
its notes. See, e.g., A. Andréadès,
A History of the Bank of England
(1909), pp. 197–202.

82   **"becomes particularly
dangerous when it is exercised
from a distance":** S. Doc. No. 173,
75th Cong., 3d Sess. 8 (1938).

83   **had to coordinate the
activities of the different actors:**
While small numbers of banks
might be able to self-coordinate
effectively, a sufficiently large
number of banks probably will
not. Any private coordinating
mechanism between large groups of
parties that do not know each other
is likely to be captured by its biggest
members.

83   **are reasonably believed to
be about to engage in:** 12 U.S.C.
§ 1818(b) (emphasis added); see also
id. § 1831p-1 (enabling rulemaking).

84   **both blaming supervisors
and enhancing their power:**
Modernizing Bank Supervision and
Regulation, Part II: Hearing Before
the Senate Committee on Banking,
Housing and Urban Affairs, 111th
Cong. 17 (2009) (Sen. Richard

Shelby) ("[Y]ou would have to give
them an 'F' . . . on their ability to
regulate the banks").

CHAPTER THREE

86   **it is best understood as a
set of multiple institutions:** see
Peter Conti-Brown, *The Power and
Independence of the Federal Reserve*
13 (2016).

86   **entitled to a periodic
dividend:** This dividend is fixed
by statute, so the member banks
are not the "residual claimants" on
the profits of the Federal Reserve
Banks. By law, those accrue to
the US Treasury, even though
the US owns no shares in the
Federal Reserve Banks. Initially,
these payments were structured
as a franchise tax. Now they are
structured as interest payments to
the Board due in connection with
their power to issue physical cash.
See United States ex rel. *Kraus v.
Wells Fargo*, 943 F.3d 588 (2d Cir.
2019).

87   **whose appointment must
also be approved by the Board:**
Until Congress passed the Dodd-
Frank Act in 2010, all nine directors
voted on the appointment of
Federal Reserve Bank presidents.
For an assessment of this complex
institutional structure and an
overview of how it has evolved
since 1913, see Peter Conti-Brown,
Power and Independence, pp. 15–39,
103–26. For an overview of how

166   Congress has amended the Federal Reserve Act over the past 108 years, see Sarah Binder & Mark Spindel, *The Myth of Independence: How Congress Governs the Federal Reserve* (2017), pp. 19–51, 93–94.

90   **to promote ... maximum employment:** FRA § 2A (codified at 12 U.S.C. 225a).

92   **"a vast concentration of power":** Senate Report No. 133, Pt. 1, 63rd Cong., 1st Sess. (November 24, 1913), p. 6.

92   **the creation of the Fed was a question of freedom:** Woodrow Wilson, Message Regarding the Banking System, June 23, 1913.

93   **"the power of life and death over American business and industry":** Cong. Rec. 4885 (1913).

93   **"so that the banks may be the instruments, not the masters":** Woodrow Wilson, Message Regarding the Banking System, June 23, 1913.

93   **"the great power of banking and currency":** Cong. Rec. 5108 (September 16, 1913) (Rep. Manahan). See also Arthur S. Link, *Wilson: The New Freedom* (1956), p. 212 (quoting letter from Louis Brandeis to Woodrow Wilson): "The power to issue currency should be vested exclusively in Government officials, even when the currency is issued against commercial paper. The American

people will not be content to have the discretion necessarily involved vested in a Board composed wholly or in part of bankers.... The conflict between the policies of the Administration and the desires of the financiers and of big business, is an irreconcilable one."

94   **"technically speaking, has no banking function":** Cong. Rec. 4645 (1913).

94   **Fed was the world's first monetary authority:** For the role played by the populist movement in creating the Fed, see Elizabeth Sanders, *Roots of Reform: Farmers, Workers, and the American State* (1999), p. 236.

98   **a constraint on the banking franchise:** See Morgan Ricks, "Money as Infrastructure," *Columbia Business Law Review* 2018, no. 3 (2019), pp. 757–851.

101   **to regulate the amount of money in the economy:** See Thomas M. Humphrey, "The Classical Concept of the Lender of Last Resort," *Federal Reserve Bank of Richmond Economic Review* (1975), pp. 2, 5.

102   **"any participant in any program or facility with broad-based eligibility":** In 1932, Congress also authorized the Fed to lend to nonbanks against treasury security collateral for short periods of time (codified at 12 U.S.C. § 347c). This authority, however, has

not been used since 1935, and the Fed has self-imposed by regulation most of the restrictions that Congress imposed by statute on 13(3) lending. See Regulation A.

CHAPTER FOUR

105 **investors have increasingly turned to alternative forms of money:** Shadow banking as a phenomenon predates the recent period. Various forms of unregulated private money creation undermined US financial stability in the pre–New Deal period. See Rockoff, "It's Always the Shadow Banks." Eliminating shadow banking was one of the goals of the New Deal banking reforms.

106 **When people lose confidence in chartered banks:** Morgan Ricks, *The Money Problem*, pp. 102–42

106 **it worsened a contraction that eventually cost the economy millions of jobs:** Regis Barnichon, Christian Matthes, and Alexander Ziegenbein, "The Financial Crisis at 10: Will We Ever Recover?" FRBSF Economic Letter (August 13, 2018).

109 **repo holders at unchartered shadow banks rarely "sell":** See Marcia Stigum, *Stigum's Money Market* (2007), pp. 531–79.

111 **the Fed offered select broker dealers access to overnight loans:** During World War II and in its initial aftermath, the Fed supported the Treasury market using its own balance sheet. In 1951, the Fed sought to free itself of this role, which it had originally taken on due to exigent circumstances. The result was an arrangement with the Truman administration known as the Fed-Treasury Accord. In my view, one of the reasons that the Fed offered dealers a backstop for their alternative form of money was to assist them in supporting the Treasury market so that the Accord would hold. In that way, the Fed used repo to substitute dealer balance sheets for its own balance sheet. This dynamic is central to Modern Monetary Theory's claim that the federal government money-finances its spending. See Nathan Tankus, "The Federal Government Always Money-Finances Its Spending: A Restatement," Notes on the Crises (June 30, 2020).

111 **"is right now doing something which I do not consider to be legal":** Hearings before the Committee on Banking and Currency, House of Representatives, 85th Cong. 1st Session on S. 1451 and H.R. 7026 (1957), pp. 1546–47.

112 **so that the Fed could more easily backstop broker dealers:** Morgan Ricks, *The Money Problem,* p. 198; Jeffrey N. Gordon and Christopher Muller, "Avoiding Eight-Alarm Fires in the Political Economy of Systemic Risk

168   Management," ECGI Working Paper Series No. 277 (2010), pp. 29–34.

112   made it easier for the broker dealers to fund themselves using repos: See generally Gordon and Muller, "Eight Alarm Fires," pp. 29–34.

114   the Fed decided to provide support for eurodollar issuers: see generally Benjamin Braun, Arie Krampf, and Steffen Murau, "Financial Globalization as Positive Integration: Monetary Technocrats and the Eurodollar Market in the 1970s," *Review of International Political Economy* 28 (2020).

116   money market funds have proved to be unstable: For an examination of how money market funds that invest in risk assets remain unstable even after post-2008 reforms, see Jeffrey N. Gordon and Christopher Gandia, "Money Market Funds Run Risk: Will Floating Net Asset Value Fix the Problem?," *Columbia Business Law Review* (2014).

117   shadow banks were issuing more money than banks: Morgan Ricks, *The Money Problem,* pp. 33–34.

119   leaving Lehman for dead and looking to hold forms of money: See Financial Stability Oversight Council, Annual Report (2011), p. 95.

CHAPTER FIVE

126   its highest since Andrew Jackson vetoed the renewal: The US system was highly decentralized until the government began to reverse restrictions on interstate branching in the 1980s and 1990s. Since 2008, the assets of the largest three commercial banks as a percentage of total commercial banking assets have hovered around 35 percent. As recently as 1997 it was just 20 percent. World Bank, Bank Concentration for United States, retrieved from FRED, Federal Reserve Bank of St. Louis (November 24, 2021). In 1817, by contrast, the Bank of the United States accounted for nearly 28 percent of the banking system as measured by equity capital. Secretary of the Treasury, Report on the Finances (1820), p. 520.

128   "It was never contemplated by Congress": Memorandum from Walter Wyatt, General Counsel of the Federal Reserve Board, to Daniel Crissinger, Governor of the Federal Reserve Board (August 18, 1923), p. 10. See also Thomas Conway and Ernest Patterson, *The Operation of the New Bank Act* (1914), p. 173 (analyzing section 14 and concluding that "a careful reading of it will show that there are a number of different ways in which the reserve banks may deal with the public" but there is "no authorization under which they may discount or lend directly to private individuals").

129   the Fed did not secure prior approval from the Treasury

Secretary: There are two provisions of Section 13 that could be used for the Fed's repo operations: Section 13(3) and Section 13(13). Section 13(3) imposes strict limits, including requiring that the Fed only lend in "unusual and exigent circumstances." Section 13(13) is more open-ended, authorizing the Fed to lend to any individual, partnership, or corporation in any circumstance, provided the loan is for no longer than ninety days and is secured by direct obligations of the United States or by obligations that are direct obligations of, or fully guaranteed as to principal and interest by, an agency of the United States. The Fed, however, has tied its own hands by imposing by regulation many of the same restrictions that exist by statute with respect to Section 13(3) to Section 13(13).

130   **What sort of facilities can the Fed characterize:** Compare Lee Reiners, "The Pandemic Relief Bill and the Battle over Federal Reserve Emergency Lending Authority," *The FinReg Blog* (December 21, 2020) (arguing that "the Fed had the legal authority—before the CARES Act—under Section 13(3) to roll out the MLF, MSLP, and the other lending programs funded by the CARES Act" and that the CARES Act confirmed this), with Jeanna Smialek, "The Year the Fed Changed Forever," *New York Times* (December 23, 2020) (explaining that Sen. Pat Toomey told the

Times that the Fed could not, going forward, use 13(3) to buy municipal bonds or make business loans without additional congressional authorization).

131   **the same sort of judicial review as the activities of other government agencies:** Fed policymaking, instead, is limited by "soft" constraints— norms developed globally among economists and central bankers. See Kathryn Judge, "The Federal Reserve: A Study in Soft Constraints," *Law and Contemporary Problems* 78 (2015), pp. 78–82. For an analysis of how the Fed's deviations from administrative law norms reduce its effectiveness, see Peter Conti-Brown, Yair Listokin, and Nicholas R. Parrillo, "Towards an Administrative Law of Central Banking," *Yale Journal on Regulation* 38 (2021).

131   **are likely to disproportionately benefit financial firms:** For an examination of the dependence of central banks like the Fed on the financial sector, see Peter Dietsch, François Claveau, and Clément Fontan, *Do Central Banks Serve the People?* (2018), pp. 46–74. See also Gerald Epstein, "Democratic Money: Central Bank Independence vs. Contested Control," Just Money (August 10, 2021).

131   **Fed staff are not trained in evaluating the credit risk:**

170   At present, the Fed also lacks a developed framework for credit policy. See Kathryn Judge, "Why the Fed Should Issue a Policy Framework for Credit Policy," Columbia Law School Working Paper No. 632 (2020).

131   **creating a "kludge":** Steven M. Teles, "Kludgeocracy in America," *National Affairs* 17 (2013), p. 97.

132   **limiting take-up, especially among smaller businesses and local governments:** See Jeanna Smialek, "A Coffee Chain Reveals Flaws in the Fed's Plan to Save Main Street," *New York Times* (July 9, 2020) (reporting that "some at Treasury saw the program as more of an absolute backstop for firms that were out of options" and that "the Treasury secretary has resisted taking on too much risk, saying at one point that he did not want to lose money on the programs").

132   **"sorely tempted to use them as informal bargaining chips over monetary policy":** Paul Tucker, *Unelected Power: The Quest For Legitimacy in Central Banking and The Regulatory State* (2018), p. 450.

133   **asset purchases affect relative prices:** See Ben Eisen and Akane Otani, "The Fed's Intervention Is Widening the Gap Between Market Haves and Have-Nots," *Wall Street Journal* (April 7, 2020).

133   **experience a wealth effect:** See Richard Cantillon, *An Essay on Economic Theory* (Mark Thorton, ed., Chantal Saucier, trans., Ludwig won Mises Institute, reprinted 2010) (1755). See also Matt Stoller, "The Cantillon Effect: Why Wall Street Gets a Bailout and You Don't," BIG (April 9, 2020).

134   **just having the Discount Window in place:** For example, Discount Window lending peaked at just $51 billion in 2020. Yale Program on Financial Stability, Key Program Summaries (2021).

134   **success as an emergency national investment authority is generally not measured:** Credit facilities like the SMCCF designed to provide market liquidity—to act as a government dealer in certain capital markets—are an exception. An announcement that the government is going to quote an outside spread in a market causes prices to appreciate immediately. See Nina Boyarchenko et al., "It's What You Say and What You Buy: A Holistic Evaluation of the Corporate Credit Facilities," Federal Reserve Bank. of New York Staff Reports, No. 935 (2020).

135   **government-backed money creation:** See Katharina Pistor, *The Code of Capital: How the Law Creates Wealth and Inequality* (2019), pp. 77–107.

135   **The financial sector . . . grew from 15 percent:** *Economic*

Report of the President (2007)
(Table B-12); Bureau of Economic
Analysis, "Value Added by Industry
as a Percentage of Gross Domestic
Product" (2021).

**135   The Fed simply cannot
distribute money democratically:**
See Craig Torres and Liz
McCormick, "Fed's 'Run It Hot'
Recipe Works for Markets. Jobs?
Not So Much," Bloomberg (June 28,
2020); Lisa Lee, "Fed Is Propping
Up Companies It Had Warned
Banks Not to Touch," Bloomberg
(May 5, 2020); David Scigliuzzo
and Julie Johnsson, "The Non-
Bailout: How the Fed Saved Boeing
Without Paying a Dime," Bloomberg
(updated May 2, 2020); Jeanna
Smialek and Deborah B. Solomon,
"A Hedge Fund Bailout Highlights
How Regulators Ignored Big Risks,"
New York Times (July 1, 2020).

**136   the Fed's QE program
inherently favored those who
owned assets:** For a critique of QE
on distributive grounds, see Peter
Dietsch, François Claveau, and
Clément Fontan, Do Central Banks
Serve the People? (2018), pp. 19–45.
For a further critique of QE and its
effect on social mobility and social
cohesion, see Lisa Adkins, Melinda
Cooper, and Martijn Konings,
The Asset Economy (2020). For a
study of how policies like QE may
contribute to the rise of right-wing
populist parties, see Ben Ansell,
Frederik Hjorth, Jacob Nyrup &
Martin Vinæs Larsen, "Sheltering

Populists? House Prices and the
Support of Populist Parties," Journal
of Politics (forthcoming).

**136   while they will not ask
questions when the Fed stretches
its statutory framework:** See,
e.g., Michael S. Derby, "Republican
Senator Wants San Francisco Fed
Documents on Climate Change and
Social Work," Wall Street Journal
(March 29, 2021); Rachel Siegel,
"Federal Reserve's Attention
to Climate Risk Draws Ire from
Republicans," Washington Post
(March 18, 2021).

**137   "lack the democratic
legitimacy to venture too far":**
Thomas Piketty, Capital and
Ideology (2020), p. 700.

**138   "Elected politicians
should not be able":** Paul Tucker,
Unelected Power, p. 436.

**139   crowd out needed legislative
action:** Paul Tucker, Unelected
Power, p. 699 ("the danger is
that these monetary policies,
by avoiding the worst, gave the
impression that no broader
structural change in social, fiscal, or
economic policy was necessary").

CHAPTER SIX

**140   Congress should attend
to the root of the problem:** As
Nathan Tankus points out, the
problem is not the Fed's large
balance sheet. See Nathan Tankus,
"The Way People Talk About the

172   Federal Reserve 'Big' Balance Sheet Is All Wrong," Notes on the Crises (July 27, 2020). The Fed's balance sheet reflects the underlying structure of our monetary system. It is, I suggest, that system that needs reforming. As outlined in this chapter, I think that reworking monetary outsourcing on more public terms is more likely to lead to better policy outcomes (that are durable) than trying to remake the Fed as a public credit modulator.

141   began to promote a new form of money to displace the dollar: See David Golumbia, *The Politics of Bitcoin: Software as Right-Wing Extremism* (2016).

141   cryptocurrencies have undercut the role of the dollar: For example, they have facilitated online ransomware attacks and illicit transactions that would have been hard or impossible to effect using existing payment rails. Justin Muzinich, "America's Crypto Conundrum," *Foreign Affairs* (November 2021).

141   their cryptographic security features consume enormous amounts of energy: Cambridge Bitcoin Electricity Consumption Index, University of Cambridge (last accessed June 6, 2021) (estimating that Bitcoin's decentralized ledger technology consumes 115 Terawatts of electricity per year, more than countries like the Netherlands and the Philippines, accounting for over 0.5 percent of worldwide electricity consumption).

143   Anyone creating products that function as securities or insurance: Morgan Ricks, *The Money Problem*, pp. 234–36.

143   might "term" out their funding: For a proposal along these lines, see Morgan Ricks, *The Money Problem*, pp. 223–47.

143   rather than using their customers' funds to invest in risky assets: See Jamie McAndrews and Lev Menand, "Shadow Digital Money"; Dan Awrey, "Bad Money," *Cornell Law Review* 106 (2020), pp. 56–69; Dan Awrey, "Unbundling Banking, Money, and Payments," *Georgetown Law Review* 110 (forthcoming 2022).

144   I have termed such money FedAccounts: John Crawford, Lev Menand, and Morgan Ricks, "FedAccounts: Digital Dollars," *George Washington Law Review* 76 (2020).

144   a CBDC that helps low-income households: Michael S. Barr et al., "Central Bank of the Future Summary and Recommendations for Further Inquiry," University of Michigan Center for Finance, Law and Policy, Paper No. 8 (2021), at pp. 23–26.

144   making it hard (if not impossible) for many households

to open and maintain bank accounts: See Aaron Klein, "A Few Small Banks Have Become Overdraft Giants," Brookings (March 1, 2021); Aaron Klein, "The Fastest Way to Address Income Inequality? Implement a Real Time Payment System," Brookings (January 2, 2019); Aaron Klein, "America's Poor Subsidize Wealthier Consumers in a Vicious Income Inequality Cycle," Brookings (February 6, 2018).

144 a failure that has prevented millions of households from building wealth: See Mehrsa Baradaran, *The Color of Money: Black Banks and the Racial Wealth Gap* (2019); Mehrsa Baradaran, *How the Other Half Banks: Exclusion, Exploitation, and the Threat to Democracy* (2015); Mehrsa Baradaran, "How the Poor Got Cut Out of Banking," *Emory Law Journal* 62 (2013); Michael S. Barr, *No Slack: The Financial Lives of Low-Income Americans* (2012).

144 could operate more effective alternatives: For federal-level proposals, see Saule T. Omarova, "Why We Need a National Investment Authority"; Robert C. Hockett and Saule T. Omarova, "Private Wealth and Public Goods: A Case for a National Investment Authority," p. 437; Robert C. Hockett and Saule T. Omarova, "White Paper: A National Investment Authority"; Mehrsa Baradaran, "It's Time for Postal Banking," *Harvard Law Review Forum* 127 (2014), p. 165. For state-level proposals, see Evan Weinberger, "California Breathes New Life into Public Banking Movement," Bloomberg Law (January 2, 2020).

145 would allow banks and shadow banks to continue operating: This was proposed during the Great Depression by a group of economists at the University of Chicago. See Ronald J. Phillips, *The Chicago Plan and New Deal Banking Reform* (1999).

145 ensuring that a lack of money is not the reason that the economy shrinks: Stephanie Kelton, *The Deficit Myth: Modern Monetary Theory and the Birth of the People's Economy* (2020).

146 whenever the three-month average unemployment rate: Claudia Sahm, "Direct Stimulus Payments to Individuals," in *Recession Ready: Fiscal Policies to Stabilize the American Economy* (2019).

147 and offering out of work people public service jobs: See Heather Boushey, Ryan Nunn, and Jay Shambaugh, *Recession Ready: Fiscal Policies to Stabilize the American Economy* (2019); Stephanie Kelton, *The Deficit Myth*, pp. 243–59 ; Yair Listokin, *Law and Macroeconomics: Legal Remedies to Recessions* (2019).

Columbia Global Reports is a publishing imprint from Columbia University that commissions authors to produce works of original thinking and on-site reporting from all over the world, on a wide range of topics. Our books are short—novella-length, and readable in a few hours—but ambitious. They offer new ways of looking at and understanding the major issues of our time. Most readers are curious and busy. Our books are for them.

Subscribe to our newsletter, and learn more about Columbia Global Reports at globalreports.columbia.edu.